JUSTICE PURSUED

UNIVERSITY PRESS OF FLORIDA

Florida A&M University, Tallahassee
Florida Atlantic University, Boca Raton
Florida Gulf Coast University, Ft. Myers
Florida International University, Miami
Florida State University, Tallahassee
New College of Florida, Sarasota
University of Central Florida, Orlando
University of Florida, Gainesville
University of North Florida, Jacksonville
University of South Florida, Tampa
University of West Florida, Pensacola

JUSTICE PURSUED

The Exoneration of Nathan Myers
and Clifford Williams

Bruce Horovitz

UNIVERSITY PRESS OF FLORIDA

Gainesville/Tallahassee/Tampa/Boca Raton
Pensacola/Orlando/Miami/Jacksonville/Ft. Myers/Sarasota

28 27 26 25 24 23   6 5 4 3 2 1

A record of the cataloging-in-publication data is available from the Library of Congress.
ISBN 978-0-8130-6988-3 (cloth)
ISBN 978-0-8130-8032-1 (pbk.)

The University Press of Florida is the scholarly publishing agency for the State University System
of Florida, comprising Florida A&M University, Florida Atlantic University, Florida Gulf Coast
University, Florida International University, Florida State University, New College of Florida, University of Central Florida, University of Florida, University of North Florida, University of South
Florida, and University of West Florida.

University Press of Florida
2046 NE Waldo Road
Suite 2100
Gainesville, FL 32609
http://upress.ufl.edu

For all who pursue justice

Contents

Author's Note

This is a book about justice. Clifford "Boonie" Williams and Nathan Myers spent just shy of forty-three years in prison for a murder they were judged not to have committed. It would be easy to see their story simply as an indictment of the criminal justice system. But it's much more than that. This story shows what happens when an imperfect system, with the noblest of intentions, works diligently to correct itself. Their eventual exoneration was the direct result of the efforts of Florida's first Conviction Integrity Review (CIR) unit, established by State Attorney Melissa Nelson in Florida's Fourth Judicial Circuit. The unit was established to review and correct wrongful convictions. Nelson is among a growing number of prosecutors establishing such units around the country.

In chronicling this story, I relied heavily on the CIR unit's investigation of the case as well as other public documents, court records, and media accounts. I interviewed several key figures involved with the exoneration as well as others with direct knowledge of the case from more than four decades ago.

All sources are noted either in the text or in the accompanying notes.

I would like to thank the State Attorney's Office of the Fourth Judicial Circuit for its cooperation and for granting access to records used in writing this book. I would also like to thank all of those interviewed for offering their recollections and perspectives. A special thanks to Nathan Myers and Clifford Williams for helping tell their story. A detailed list of those who contributed can be found in the book's acknowledgments.

1

Introduction

By age seventeen, Hubert "Nathan" Myers was already a marked man.

In the segregated streets of Jacksonville, Florida, Nathan was guilty by association. His uncle, Clifford "Boonie" Williams Jr., was well known to law enforcement as a drug dealer, gang leader, and convicted felon. Nathan, a high school football star with a promising future, could not escape his uncle's shadow. Nor could he pull himself away from the lifestyle his uncle offered the teenager, managing the neighborhood pool hall and driving around town in a fancy Cadillac Eldorado with a beige top.

It all came crashing down in the wee morning hours of May 2, 1976, when shots rang out deep in the heart of Jacksonville's inner city, where drugs, alcohol, and gun violence ruled the day. Another presumed "Black on Black" shooting in a city notorious for its homicide rate.

Less than two hours after the shooting, Nathan Myers and his uncle Clifford Williams were arrested for the murder of Jeanette "Baldie" Williams (no relation), who was killed after sustaining multiple bullet wounds while in bed with her partner, Nina Marshall. Marshall was also wounded but escaped the scene and made it to a nearby hospital. It was there that she identified the shooters as Myers and Williams.

Never mind that more than thirty witnesses confirmed that Myers and Williams were attending a neighborhood party when the shots were heard. Never mind that both men, who proclaimed their innocence, were found to be clean of any gunpowder residue shortly after the shooting. Never mind that the crime scene bore little resemblance to Nina Marshall's eyewitness account of how the shooting went down. Within a few months, Myers and Williams were tried for first-degree murder and attempted murder. They were found guilty in a trial lasting only two days. Both ended up with life sentences. (Williams was originally sentenced to death, but the Florida Supreme Court overturned his death sentence by a single vote, 4–3, in 1980.)

What transpired over the forty-three years since the shooting is a case study of the sometimes-flawed criminal justice system, with its rush to judgment, racial overtones, and forensic evolution. It is, however, ultimately a story of redemption, resulting in the release from prison of both Myers and Williams on March 28, 2019, in a landmark case initiated by the very office that prosecuted them more than four decades ago. Unlike so many other overturned convictions, it was not new DNA evidence that resulted in the exoneration but rather an exhaustive reinvestigation of the evidence in the case by the state's first Conviction Integrity Review (CIR) unit. It marked the first time in Florida history that a murder conviction reversal was initiated by the prosecution.[1] The forty-two-year, eleven-month incarceration of Myers and Williams was, at the time, the fourth-longest in recorded history before an exoneration.[2]

Beyond the historical implications is the human story of Nathan Myers and Clifford Williams. Their time served for a murder they were ultimately judged not to have committed took an incalculable personal toll on the two men and their families. For Myers, it was his adolescent judgments and family history that led him to the wrong place at the wrong time, resulting in his spending the majority of his life behind bars. This is the story of his own personal transformation in an often-corrupt prison environment that offered little if any hope. Myers's ongoing faith in a system that put him in jail in the first place but ultimately secured his freedom is a testament to his perseverance and faith in the face of arguably inadequate representation. When he entered prison at age eighteen, Nathan Myers was barely an adult. He emerged a man at age sixty-one, hardened, but grateful and committed to his Christian faith and to making the most of his newfound freedom as an advocate and role model for others. His first taste of freedom was to get down on both knees and kiss the ground under his feet.

For Clifford Williams, prison was not a new experience. He had previously served time for robbery and attempted arson. This time he found himself initially on death row for a murder he said he did not commit. Williams also left prison transformed by his faith in God and grateful for his freedom. At age seventy-six however, he emerged tired and weak with an aggressive prostate cancer that went undiagnosed during his incarceration and that would require immediate medical treatment.

Their release from prison was a seminal event. But it wasn't the end of their legal battles.

Both would seek compensation for time spent (and lost) in prison. Their case would become a bipartisan hinge point for the Florida Legislature, resulting in a vigorous reexamination of the Sunshine State's laws governing compensation for wrongful convictions. Newspaper headlines across Florida hailed their story while legislators offered poignant public apologies for how the two men had been mistreated. They were given standing ovations in the legislative chambers and elevated to a hero-like status.

The exoneration of Myers and Williams was also a major political and judicial win for State Attorney Melissa Nelson, once dubbed "the most powerful woman in Northeast Florida" after her meteoric rise in the election of 2016, when she defeated the incumbent state attorney, Angela Corey, by a whopping 38 percent in the Republican Party primary.[3] Describing herself as "tough but fair," Nelson established Florida's first CIR unit in 2018.[4] The stated goal was "eliminating wrongful convictions in our community."[5]

To run the unit, Nelson appointed a veteran defense attorney, Shelley Thibodeau, to identify and investigate wrongful convictions and advocate to have them vacated.

Among the legal experts who helped Nelson establish the CIR unit was a high-profile Jacksonville defense attorney, Hank Coxe, a former president of the Florida Bar Association. Coxe had been instrumental in convincing Nelson to run for state attorney.

In an ironic and awkward twist, it was Coxe who originally prosecuted Myers and Williams as a young, zealous assistant state attorney in 1976. He had no idea the first case the CIR unit would help overturn would be his own.

The release of Myers and Williams received high public accolades in a state with a poor record of wrongful convictions. Florida has more exonerations of death row inmates than any other state in the country.[6] The case of Myers and Williams was a victory for advocacy groups like the Innocence Project of Florida and for the law firm Holland & Knight, both of which provided pro bono assistance with the exoneration and helped secure compensation for the wrongful convictions.

There remain those who, despite an exhaustive reinvestigation and the court's findings, still question the innocence of Myers and Williams. They argue that while there may have been flaws related to their conviction, nothing uncovered during the reinvestigation proved their innocence.

Some in law enforcement have challenged the wisdom of spending valuable dollars and resources from the State Attorney's Office on reopening a case tried in front of a jury more than four decades ago, when the same resources could be applied to battling an ongoing crime epidemic. Moreover, couldn't these funds be better used to prevent wrongful convictions from happening in the first place?

Despite its eventual outcome, this is by no means a sanitized story. By their own admission and criminal record, Myers and Williams were hardly saints at the time of their arrest. Especially Williams, a convicted felon with an extensive rap sheet. The same holds true for some of the victims, eyewitnesses, and others involved in this tangled saga. They were not unlike many others growing up in housing projects in the Deep South, where guns, drugs, and gang violence were a way of life. But their story is real, and it points in all directions to the complex issues of the justice system in America.

The alarming rate of wrongful convictions in the United States has given rise to a whole new industry—exoneration work. According to the National Registry of Exonerations, there have been more than 3,300 exonerations in the United States since 1989.[7] The numbers have increased dramatically since 2011.

"There are more innocent people in our jails and prisons today than ever before," reports the Equal Justice Initiative, a private, nonprofit organization that provides legal representation to those who have been wrongfully convicted.[8]

A study funded by the Department of Justice estimates the rate of wrongful convictions is up to 11.6 percent, or more than 230,000 individuals held in prisons throughout the United States.[9] And research by the National Academy of Sciences reports that 4 percent of people on death row are there because of "erroneous convictions."[10]

Advances in DNA testing, the emergence of social media, and the efforts of judicial advocacy groups like the Innocence Project and the Equal Justice Initiative have brought a new level of awareness and hope to those serving time in prison for crimes for which they were wrongfully convicted.

Some defense firms now have dedicated departments specializing in pro bono exoneration work. There is even a national trend among prosecutors to prioritize their "ethical commitment" to justice to review past convictions. This effort has resulted in a rapid proliferation of CIR units being established inside the walls of district attorney offices.

"The rate of exonerations continues to rise, revealing an unreliable system of criminal justice," according to the Equal Justice Initiative (EJI).[11] The EJI cites a lack of accountability, inadequate representation, and mistaken eyewitness identification as major contributors.[12] "More than half of wrongful convictions can be traced to eyewitnesses who lied in court or made false accusations," reports the EJI.[13]

The past few decades have seen no shortage of high-profile exonerations that have made headlines, shedding more public light on the issue. Some have become the subjects of award-winning documentaries, television series, and best-selling books.

Walter McMillian, a forty-five-year-old Black, self-employed logger, was exonerated and released from death row in 1993, when new evidence determined he was innocent of the murder of a young white woman in Monroeville, Alabama, in 1988. He was among the first exonerees from death row in the modern era.[14] His story became the centerpiece of the *New York Times* bestseller *Just Mercy*, written by civil rights attorney Bryan Stevenson, founder of the EJI. The movie adaptation, starring Michael B. Jordan and Jamie Foxx, grossed more than $50 million at the box office.[15]

The Central Park Five, charged with the rape and assault of a female jogger, had their convictions vacated in 2002 as a result of DNA testing. Their exoneration became the subject of a Ken Burns documentary, an opera, and a television miniseries. New York City named a gate in Central Park the "Gate of Exoneration" in honor of the five men. The story of the five Black and Hispanic teenagers exposed, in vivid detail, the dynamics of coerced confessions.[16]

Of course, on the other side of these high-profile success stories are the less-publicized examples of an accused being released from prison on a legal technicality or an appeal only to commit additional crimes, sometimes even more heinous, upon their release. After all, prisons are for criminals. And just because a court determines someone was "wrongfully convicted" doesn't automatically mean they are "factually innocent." Yet, there is no denying that the innocent sometimes fall victim to an imperfect system.

Given their high rate of incarceration, it should come as no surprise that African Americans also account for 47 percent of exonerations, even though they represent only 13 percent of the population, according to a 2017 study conducted by the National Registry of Exonerations.[17] (The percentage is even higher for those exonerated through DNA evidence; see appendix B.) While not identifying a single cause for this disparity, it cited several reasons, including the high homicide rates in the African American community and the fact that Blacks are more often stopped, searched, and questioned than whites.[18]

Others are disadvantaged as well.

"Children and people with mental disabilities are especially vulnerable to being wrongfully convicted," reports the EJI.[19]

The legal battle to pursue an exoneration can be prolonged, expensive, and, often, futile. As author, attorney, and Innocence Project board member John Grisham notes, "Once an innocent person is convicted it is next to impossible to get them out of prison."[20]

The justice system affords all accused the protection of a presumption of innocence, with the burden of proof "beyond a reasonable doubt" squarely on the shoulders of the prosecution. However, once convicted by a jury, that presumption of innocence is gone, forever. Courts have found jury verdicts to be impregnable, and appeals are primarily limited to matters of law, not facts.[21]

There is an abiding faith, supported over time, that the system works and that juries get it right, which they undoubtedly do most of the time. But, as the growing number of exonerations show, sometimes they don't, through no fault of their own. In some cases, new evidence comes to light years after a conviction.

There is a long history of prosecutors reinvestigating questionable convictions and obtaining exonerations. Prosecutors are not in the business of convicting innocent people.

The recent emergence of CIR units headed by district attorneys is a further testament to their ongoing commitment to justice and has added a new dimension to the landscape of wrongful convictions. Utilizing the power of the State and its resources to review past convictions has leveled a playing field usually reserved for pro bono defense attorneys.

"Thus, it turns the common concept of 'David versus Goliath' around to approach the problem from the context of what if Goliath develops a social justice conscience?" observed LeRoy Pernell, law professor and former dean of Florida A&M Law School.[22]

Behind every violent crime are the human faces, the personal stories, and the unique circumstances that set it apart. Each case provides yet another opportunity to administer justice or, when appropriate, to correct an injustice.

This is one such story.

2

Consolidation

On October 1, 1968, Jacksonville, Florida, officially began its bold experiment of a consolidated government. A new law approved by voters one year earlier had gone into effect. Overnight the Northeast Florida community on the banks of the St. Johns River that was once known as "Cowford" had suddenly become the largest city in land area in the contiguous United States. As a result of the new consolidation plan, Jacksonville had exploded from 39 square miles to 840. It jumped from the seventy-fifth-most-populated city to the twenty-seventh.[1]

The move to consolidate the city and county government was a long time in the making. The idea of Jacksonville annexing surrounding suburbs within Duval County had been voted on before but had been rejected each time. By the 1960s, Jacksonville was not unlike a lot of other southern cities experiencing the pressures of "white flight" to the suburbs that had escalated following World War II. The impact was a declining tax base for the core city, which was beginning to run out of money for the basic yet critical essentials like sanitation and education. Meanwhile, Duval County's government acted independently from the city but had limited resources to serve the rapidly growing population outside the city limits.[2]

The result was a dysfunctional and corrupt government. In November 1966, eleven city officials, including four city council members, were indicted on 142 counts of bribery and larceny.[3] Two years earlier, in 1964, all fifteen Duval County high schools were disaccredited, following years of underfunding.[4] In that same year, the city received some unwelcome publicity when the Beatles threatened to cancel their September 11 Gator Bowl concert after learning the audience would be segregated. Former Beatle Paul McCartney recalled the showdown in a 2020 Instagram post:

In 1964 The Beatles were due to play Jacksonville in the US and we found out that it was going to be to a segregated audience. It felt wrong. We said, "We're not doing that!"[5]

The Beatles insisted an integrated audience be included as part of their contract, and the show went on as scheduled. (As it turned out, the newly enacted Civil Rights Act would have legally required the audience to be integrated.)[6] The showdown was prominently featured in Ron Howard's 2016 documentary *Eight Days a Week*.

By the mid-1960s, the city's reputation was becoming as pungent as the odor emanating from its pulp mills.

Many city leaders saw consolidation as the answer. Other Florida cities like Miami and Tampa made similar attempts to create consolidated governments but failed. Jacksonville, however, was poised and ready.

Championed by a former Southern Bell Telephone executive, Claude Yates, an aggressive campaign was launched to convince voters and the Florida Legislature of the pressing need to consolidate the city and county governments.[7] Inner-city residents were promised a greater voice in the newly formed government that had been purged of corruption and cronyism (although some argued consolidation was a move directed at keeping Blacks out of office by expanding voting to the predominately white suburbs). Suburbanites were lured by the economic benefits and efficiencies of unified services.[8]

On August 8, 1967, more than 86,000 voters went to the polls and voted overwhelmingly (almost 2 to 1) in favor of consolidation.[9] Jacksonville had done what no other southern city had been able to accomplish. Many locals believed the consolidation plan would soon become a model for urban political reform in the 1970s.

City leaders began touting Jacksonville as the "Bold New City of the South," using the campaign slogan of the consolidation movement.[10] As promised, consolidation delivered on many fronts, including a much-needed financial boost bolstered by the economic efficiencies of unified public services and a broad tax base. Jacksonville, as a gateway to Florida, became one of the South's most marketable cities, attracting big names like the Mayo Clinic, the PGA Tour, and even landing an NFL franchise in 1997. Against all odds, the city with one of the smallest NFL markets was selected to host the 2005 Super Bowl with Paul McCartney, who once threatened a Beatles boycott, as the halftime entertainment. And the city whose deep-seated segregation habits were slow to unwind elected the affable Nat

Glover in 1995 as the first Black sheriff in Florida since the end of Reconstruction. In 2011, Democrat Alvin Brown became Jacksonville's first Black mayor, albeit for one term.

But not everyone benefited from the paradigm shift. From its early days, consolidation failed to deliver on many of the promises made to the inner city, which had supported the effort. The same benefits and quality services afforded new construction developments in the sprawling suburbs did not find their way to the city's older, inner core.[11] Promises to improve conditions failed to pan out. As early as 1973 a Jacksonville University study found that spending patterns showed "the have-nots and the minorities did not win on the more controversial issues involving significant costs to segments of the community."[12]

Blighted areas in the Black community in particular showed no signs of progress. Housing projects like Blodgett Homes in the city's Northside neighborhood saw little if any improvement in living conditions or economic opportunity.

Consolidation's goal of easing the urban-suburban divide did little to address the long-standing issues of racism, poverty, and socioeconomic inequality. The suburbs may have been expanding, but the inner city was festering with drugs, gang wars, and violence. More than one city official described Jacksonville as a "tale of two cities."[13]

Half a century later many are still waiting. *Florida Times-Union* columnist Nate Monroe described it this way:

"What happened, by now, is a familiar story in this town: The white establishment broke its promise, then did it again and again and again and now it has been a generation and many of these neighborhoods are still waiting for basic services like the city water lines they were promised a half century ago. . . . This can't be said enough: In Jacksonville the failure to achieve equality is the direct result of an unfulfilled promise."[14]

The inner city still struggles with violent crime, unable to shed its unenviable label as the "murder capital of Florida." Even during the early days of the coronavirus pandemic in 2020, Duval County bucked the national trend. While "sheltering in place" resulted in a nationwide reduction in violent crimes, Jacksonville's murder rate actually increased.[15]

"Sadly, frankly, since COVID-19, our shootings and homicide rates have escalated," State Attorney Melissa Nelson testified to a presidential commission on law enforcement on April 8, 2020.[16]

For decades, much of the violence centered around "Black on Black" crime in Northwest Jacksonville, where gangs and drugs were prevalent.

Despite these disturbing trends, the establishment's argument is that consolidation has done more good than bad. But as far back as its early years there were warning signs that consolidation was having little effect on life in the inner city.

There had been progress, for sure, but the Bold New City of the South was still very much a segregated town in the mid-1970s despite the promises of a bold new consolidated government.

3

Boomerang

While Jacksonville was experimenting with its new consolidated government, Clifford "Boonie" Williams was presiding over one of the more ancient forms of rule, a kind of feudalism prevalent in drug-related gangs.

"We had some soldiers, lieutenants and things all over town," Williams recalled. "I had a big dope ring at the time, the Boomerang Gang."[1] They ran along Jacksonville's inner core from Ashley Street to East Florida Avenue to Twenty-First Street. Their neighborhoods included Mixon Town and Brooklyn. The Boomerangs dealt in drugs and guns.[2]

"We had kilos of dope . . . heroin, cocaine, we had it all," said Williams.[3]

More than a half century later, Williams is a shell of the man once known as a drug-dealing thug and neighborhood bully with little respect for the law. Forty-three years in prison, health issues, and a return to his religious roots have softened his demeanor and changed his outlook on life.

Small in stature, he is soft-spoken, unsteady, and not always clear in his memory. He speaks openly about his faith in God and is quick to express his gratitude for his newfound freedom. One would be hard-pressed to look at him today and envision the hardened criminal who ruled the Boomerang Gang in the 1970s. Nevertheless, he described those turbulent years as "an exciting time."[4]

The Boomerangs were not new to Jacksonville. Long before they became involved in criminal activity, the Black street gang was born out of the racial tensions of the civil rights movement of the 1960s.

"The name Boomerang refers to the idea of what goes around comes around, that the chickens come home to roost," wrote Jacksonville author Tim Gilmore.[5]

The Boomerang Gang played a major role in one of the darkest days in Jacksonville history. On August 27, 1960, the Youth Council of the National Association for the Advancement of Colored People (NAACP) was participating in a peaceful protest, sitting at a "whites only" lunch counter, when they were spit upon by white attackers yelling racial slurs. More than two hundred whites, armed with baseball bats and ax handles, began chasing the young protestors through the streets of Jacksonville as police stood by and watched. When the Boomerang Gang attempted to protect those being beaten, the police joined the melee, adding their nightsticks to the baseball bats and ax handles. The bloody incident became notoriously known as "Ax Handle Saturday."[6] (Before it was canceled due to COVID-19 concerns, President Donald Trump was scheduled to receive his party's nomination for a second term in Jacksonville on the sixtieth anniversary of Ax Handle Saturday. The last-minute cancellation avoided a likely confrontation between planned demonstrations commemorating the event and the Republican National Convention.)

By the time Clifford Williams joined up with the Boomerangs, it had evolved into a violent street gang dealing in drugs and guns.

Williams had grown up in a neighborhood known as "Black Bottom" near Clay and Broad Streets in downtown Jacksonville. He was one of eleven children. It was a rough neighborhood, according to Williams. "I would say it was a lot like Harlem in New York," he recalled.[7]

It was nevertheless a close-knit community where families and friends stuck together. Among Williams's closest friends in the neighborhood was Eddie Lee Rosemond and his sister Leatrice, who decades later would become Williams's wife.[8]

"We were like the Three Musketeers," he mused.[9]

Clifford was known as a neighborhood charmer.[10] Despite being raised in a religious home where he was expected in church every Sunday morning, Williams acknowledged he and Eddie Lee got in a lot of trouble that would eventually lead them both into a high-stakes life of crime.[11] He dropped out of school before completing the eighth grade and would be arrested more than twenty-five times for various crimes including attempted arson, assault, and drug trafficking.[12]

It's a lifestyle Williams now regrets.

"Back then it was a matter of survival," he said. In a climate of everyday gang warfare, it was "kill or be killed."[13]

Williams's first major run-in with the law came at age sixteen. It was over a slap.

"This dude slapped me because I made one of my soldiers beat his cousin's behind," is how Williams remembered it. The confrontation took place in front of a phone booth on Ashley Street in downtown Jacksonville. Williams was armed with a nine-shot .38 caliber pistol.

"I knew someone was going to get foolish with me, and I had a hell of a temper back then," Williams said. "The dude had a knife."[14]

As he was being forced into the phone booth at knifepoint, Williams said, he pulled his gun, which was hiding up his sleeve. "I said, 'No, no, tough guy,' and I kept shooting until it was empty."[15]

An eyewitness testified that the shooting was done in self-defense, and the sixteen-year-old Williams walked out a free man. "I beat the case, but that was the beginning of trouble."[16]

Over the next several years Williams and his best friend, Eddie Lee, spent time in prison and running from police as they engaged in an extensive drug-trafficking ring with the help of the Boomerang Gang.

It was a violent but lucrative lifestyle that extended well beyond the boundaries of Jacksonville. Williams said he dealt with drug lords from Detroit to Miami.[17]

He spent the money as fast as he could make it.

"I spent a lot of money going to jail and other things," he said.[18]

In addition to the drugs there were guns, and lots of them, including Russian-made machine guns. "We had gang wars; you had to have guns," Williams said emphatically.[19]

Whether Williams's recollections are simply bravado or real is hard to know. But his activity as a drug dealer is undisputed.

Williams said neither he nor his partner Rosemond used the hard drugs they were trafficking. "But I did love that reefer," he said.[20]

His criminal activities put Williams squarely in the crosshairs of the local police radar. Even with his frequent arrests, many times the charges failed to stick and he was released.

"I was lucky I didn't get caught by the Feds, but I kind of managed to stay away from them," Williams said. He was found guilty of a felony only twice; of attempted arson in 1960 and of armed robbery in 1965.[21]

Williams carried on extramarital affairs and kept company with some whom police at the time described as "admitted homosexuals."[22] He set up shop at an old laundromat that had been converted to a pool hall near the corner of Davis and First Streets in Jacksonville. In addition to several pool tables, the "Eight Ball" pool room had a jukebox and a small convenience store. It was at the pool hall that Williams's nephew Hubert "Nathan" Myers began spending time during his high school years.

"You know, I really tried to keep Nate away from me because he had real potential," Williams said of his young nephew.[23]

Nathan Myers grew up in the crime-riddled Blodgett Homes neighborhood, a 654-unit public housing project. He excelled on his high school football team, playing linebacker for the Sandalwood Saints in the early 1970s. Weighing in at more than two hundred pounds, Myers was a neighborhood hero with his own fan club of admirers who would attend his Friday-night games on the gridiron. Part of his appeal was that he also drove an Eldorado Cadillac to and from school. The fancy ride was a gift from his drug-dealing uncle, Clifford Williams, whose sister was Nathan Myers's mother.[24] Clifford took care of his family with the money he was making in the illicit drug business.

"I was living large," Myers remembered. "People didn't think I was going to graduate because I was on the loose end, smoking pot, running wild." He professed that while he liked smoking pot, he stayed away from hard drugs.[25]

Like his uncle, Myers, too, is open to talking about his past. Despite spending most of his life in prison, Myers has stayed in top condition. He looks strong and healthy. He has amazing recall down to the most minute details. He is articulate, determined, and wedded to his faith and his wife, Rose, whom he married while in prison. His memories of his high school years and beyond are vivid and colorful if not always pleasant.

After a stellar high school football career, Myers had his heart set on playing college ball at the University of Tampa. He idolized Freddie Solomon, the soon to be NFL star who played quarterback for the University of Tampa Spartans. Solomon would go on to play eleven seasons in the NFL as a standout receiver for the Miami Dolphins and the San Francisco 49ers.

"They had a good team coming up there next year, and the coach said I had a good chance to start because I was bigger than the linebacker they had coming back," Myers said.[26]

As he awaited word on a potential football scholarship at the University of Tampa, the school unexpectedly announced it was dropping its successful football program after the 1974 season because it could not afford the cost of competing in NCAA Division 1A football. Contributing to that decision was the arrival of the new Tampa Bay Buccaneers NFL franchise.

"It broke my heart," Myers said. "I wanted to play so bad for the Tampa Spartans."

Other scholarship offers came his way from Georgia Tech and Ole Miss, but Myers said the racial tensions in the South were a deciding factor in his decision to forgo college and stay home in Jacksonville. It was a decision that did not sit well with his mother or other family friends.[27]

"When they [University of Tampa] disbanded football, it discouraged me from going anywhere else," Myers said. "So, I failed like a lot of other Black kids. I fell down the street hustling, busy doing stuff I got no business doing. That was my lifestyle as a teenager."[28]

But for Nathan, it was a lifestyle with some benefits, thanks in part to his uncle Clifford. Williams let Myers run the pool hall and in turn kept his nephew supplied with some of the luxuries in life, including fancy cars, hotel rooms around town, and an apartment on Morgan Street.

His close association with his uncle kept him on the police radar, too.

"They were picking on me because of my uncle's history," Myers said of the police.

He recalled being pulled over on numerous occasions because police knew the Eldorado he was driving around town belonged to Williams. "I feel like I was harassed because they knew it was his car."[29]

Myers had his own run-ins with law enforcement. Once, he and a passenger were pulled over and while police were searching for drugs, they found a gun hidden under the seat. Myers was arrested, but the passenger eventually told police that the gun was his and not Myers's.

His most significant incident came when, at age seventeen, he was followed by police who saw him carrying a brown bag into the pool hall. "The police thought I was carrying drugs," Myers said. "I told them I don't mess with no drugs." Williams, who had been down the street, noticed the police presence at his pool hall and confronted the officers.[30]

"He said, 'you got no reason to be in my business,'" Myers recalled. "One officer came up from behind and grabbed my uncle in a choke hold. Well, I just kind of snapped and I dived in on everybody. I was fighting with the police and a big brawl broke out."[31]

He ended up going to jail, but the charges were dropped. "They didn't have no evidence against me," Myers said. "All they saw was a brown paper bag. When they looked in the bag they didn't find nothing . . . so, I got away."[32]

The police, who were trying to crack down on the incessant drug and gang activity in the area, had their hands full with the likes of Williams, Myers, and their associates, who, with a few exceptions, seemed to have a knack for slipping through the system.

It would all come to a head on a humid May night in 1976 in a murder that would become a landmark case in Florida legal and judicial history.

4

Murder

Clifford Williams and Nathan Myers make no bones about their criminal past.

Both fully acknowledge their frequent run-ins with law enforcement.

"I guess sometimes you have to pay for something you did, with something you didn't do," Williams mused.[1]

As summer approached in 1976, there was nothing particularly remarkable going on in Jacksonville. Like most cities, it was preparing for the nation's Bicentennial. Jimmy Carter had just edged out George Wallace in the Florida primary, and the city was laying plans for "The Biggest Concert of Summer '76" featuring the Who in the venerable Gator Bowl at twelve dollars a ticket.[2]

Consolidation had done little to ease the festering crime problems and sordid living conditions in the inner city. Economic hardships being felt nationwide put a strain on public services. The Jacksonville Sheriff's Office had been hit especially hard with a hiring freeze and was having to implement strict control of its resources despite a growth in the crime rate.[3] The city's top cop, Sheriff Dale Carson, adopted a philosophy aimed at continuing to provide sufficient police services under adverse conditions: "Support of a few good men through technological innovations and advance [sic] police techniques which provide high degrees of mobility, flexibility and safety as well as command and control is essential."[4]

Carson, a former FBI agent, served as Jacksonville's sheriff for nearly three decades. He was known nationally in law enforcement circles and in 1977 was on a short list of three candidates being considered for FBI director to succeed the retiring Clarence Kelly.[5] He was appointed Duval County sheriff by Governor LeRoy Collins in 1958. Under the consolidation plan implemented in 1968, Carson became sheriff of the largest city in land area in the United States. The legendary lawman was an innovator in upgrading training and standards for police officers. Voters reelected Carson seven times.[6]

Policing the country's largest city in land area was a challenge, especially in the face of budgetary restrictions. A 1975 FBI publication showed Jacksonville ranked twenty-second in population but forty-ninth in the number of police officers per 1,000 population.[7]

Sheriff Carson blamed much of the violence on Jacksonville's streets on "uncontrolled prostitution and rampant homosexual activity," which he described as a "cancer that can and will destroy a community."[8]

In 1976, there were ninety murders in Jacksonville.[9]

One of those homicides would take place in the early-morning hours of May 2, 1976, at 1550 Morgan Street in the New Town neighborhood of Jacksonville. The apartment was the scene of drug activity and a twisted web of multiple romantic rendezvous.

Among those living in the apartment at the time of the murder were two women, Jeanette "Baldie" Williams and Nina Marshall, who were in a romantic relationship. Before Nina moved in, Jeanette had been sharing the first-floor apartment with Christine Mitchell, a known drug dealer. Mitchell was having an affair with Clifford Williams (who was married at the time) when she was sent to jail for possession of heroin in 1975. Because she had been seeing Clifford, she was also familiar with his young nephew Nathan, who would often visit the apartment. When she was sent off to prison, Mitchell asked her boyfriend Clifford and his nephew Nathan to keep an eye on the apartment and handle rent and other matters. Both were given keys to the apartment building.[10]

In the early part of 1976, during Mitchell's incarceration, Jeanette Williams began a relationship with Nina Marshall, who had just finished serving her own prison sentence on drug charges. Sometime during the spring of 1976, Nina Marshall moved into the Morgan Street apartment and began sharing a room with Jeanette Williams. Jeanette worked at a carwash; Nina was unemployed. Nina sold drugs and engaged in prostitution to support her ongoing heroin habit.[11]

Nathan Myers, who was running his uncle's pool hall, began staying at the two-bedroom Morgan Street apartment, where he said he struck up a close friendship with Jeanette Williams.

"We were like brothers and sisters," Myers said. "She would cook special meals for me on Sundays. I loved her collard greens and macaroni and cheese."[12]

Late in the evening of Saturday, May 1, and into the next morning, a birthday party was being held for Rachel Jones at her apartment located at 1604 Morgan Street, about fifty yards down the street from the apartment where Jeanette Williams, Nina Marshall, and Nathan Myers were living. There were four identical concrete apartment buildings on the block, all quadruplexes, side by side with two apartments on the first floor and two on the second floor.[13]

Jones was gay, as were many of the other Black women who lived on the block. It was a close-knit neighborhood, and everyone chipped in to buy food and drinks for the party.[14]

At around 1:00 a.m., Clifford Williams; his pregnant wife, Barbara; Nathan Myers; Raymond "Rico" Rivers; and Rosetta "Cookie" Simmon arrived at the party.[15]

"I never would have went to that party," Myers insisted. "But my uncle said we needed to go because these were friends of ours."[16]

There were thirty to forty people at the birthday celebration all packed into Rachel Jones's apartment at 1604 Morgan Street. Sometime between 1:30 a.m. and 2:00 a.m. the partygoers described hearing what sounded like gunfire.[17]

"We thought somebody had gotten drunk and was cutting up down there," Myers recalled. "So, we went back to eating. One of the neighbors came down and said, 'Man you got the police and rescue down at your house.'"[18]

Myers said he and several others who were attending the party went down the street to see what was happening. It was there that he found a police officer at the front door of his apartment.

Myers recalled the exchange as follows:

Myers: "Excuse me sir, what's going on here?"

Officer: "Well, we got a big problem here."

Myers: "What do you mean we got a problem? My name is Nathan Myers and I live here."

Officer: "I'm going to tell you what's going on here. We got a body. One girl dead, another girl in the hospital. Do you think you can identify the body?"

Myers said he went inside the apartment and found Jeanette Williams lying dead in her bed.

He said he was distraught. "I went back outside and told the crowd, 'My God that's Baldie in there dead,'" Myers said.[19]

Police reports show that Patrolman John Zipperer was first on the scene, arriving at 2:30 a.m. Earlier that evening Zipperer had worked security at a Lynyrd Skynyrd concert at the Jacksonville Memorial Coliseum. "After the concert I had to go home, take a shower, and put on a clean uniform because of all the marijuana they had been smoking at the concert," Zipperer recalled. On his way back to the police station, Zipperer heard a call on his police radio about a possible shooting on Morgan Street. Since he was less than a block away, he headed to the scene.[20]

"At that time, we were policemen," Zipperer said. "We didn't wait on backup."

Zipperer said he entered the apartment and followed bloody footprints to a rear bedroom where a Black female was lying in the bed apparently dead.[21]

"I yelled at her. She didn't respond," Zipperer said. "She had a couple of bullet holes in her. The bed was covered with blood." He tried to get a pulse, but there was none.[22]

Zipperer conjectured there may have been a second victim, based on bloody footprints leading away from the apartment. He radioed in his findings and was soon joined by several other officers including lead investigator Richard C. Bowen of the Jacksonville Sheriff's Office.[23]

Jeanette Williams, age thirty, had been in bed with her lover, Nina Marshall, when the shooting occurred. Marshall, age twenty-six, was wounded but managed to leave the apartment after the shooting to seek help. She flagged down a passing car driven by Harold Torrence, who took her to nearby University Hospital.

Police Officer K. C. Monroe was at University Hospital on another case when Marshall arrived at the emergency room with her gunshot wounds. While he began interrogating Marshall in the emergency room, other officers were interviewing witnesses near or at the crime scene who had been attending Rachel Jones's birthday party.[24]

Both Myers and Williams were interviewed and stated they were at the party when they and other partygoers heard the gunfire. This was confirmed by Rachel Jones, who told police that both Myers and Williams were indeed at her party. The statements of other witnesses given during the night of the murder (and during pretrial depositions) painted a consistent picture.[25]

The witnesses all recalled both Myers and Williams getting a plate of food from the kitchen shortly after their arrival around 1:00 a.m. and that Williams's pregnant wife, Barbara, was seated in the kitchen. The witnesses interviewed said they heard what sounded like a series of loud gunshots and that Clifford Williams went out to the porch to see what happened before coming back inside. The witnesses recalled Nathan Myers was sitting in the living room when the shots were heard. Many of the partygoers including Myers and Williams then went down the block when they realized police had arrived at the 1550 Morgan Street apartment. No one interviewed saw either Williams or Myers leave the apartment prior to the shots being heard.[26]

Meanwhile, Nina Marshall was telling Officer Monroe a different story as she lay wounded and awaiting surgery at University Hospital. Doctors observed that Marshall had suffered three gunshot wounds. The first bullet had entered just below her left body cavity and had exited out the anterior of her neck. The second bullet had entered her left side near her voice box and had exited through her right side. A third wound was identified in her left forearm, where a bullet remained.[27] Barely able to speak, Marshall communicated with Officer Monroe that she had been shot by Clifford Williams and Nathan Myers. With a borrowed pencil she scribbled three separate notes that read: "Clifford Williams"; "Nathan"; and "go see about Jeanette Williams." She offered no other specific information at that time.[28]

Officer Monroe said he was familiar with the name "Clifford Williams" and kept his mugshot in his vehicle, which he showed to Nina Marshall, who identified him as one of the shooters.[29]

Back at the crime scene, police were gathering evidence. Jeanette Williams had been found facedown on the bed. Detectives noticed a hole in the screen of the bedroom window and that the glass pane was broken. There was glass in the bed. The screen and the window were taken in as evidence. Although they noted small holes in the curtains hanging from the window, the curtains were not collected. No fingerprints were found outside the window. Police recovered two bullets inside, one on the mattress and one on the floor underneath the bedroom window.

Except for the blood that had pooled on the mattress and floor, the bedroom appeared mostly undisturbed.[30]

While processing the crime scene, police received a communication from Officer Monroe at University Hospital that Nina Marshall had identified the shooters as Clifford "Boonie" Williams and Nathan Myers.[31]

"I knew 'Boonie' and Nate because they were in the dope business," Police Officer Zipperer recalled. "There were a lot of heroin dealers back in the day, and it was something we were always concerned with."[32]

At approximately 3:00 a.m., police handcuffed and arrested Clifford Williams, who was still outside among the group of partygoers. As he was being taken away, Williams asked that someone call his attorney and make a list of the people who had been at the party.

While he was being transported to jail, Williams told Police Officer Doyle O'Bryant that "he was at the party, he's got lots of witnesses to prove he was at the party down the street and that he was nowhere near that place."[33]

As his uncle was being arrested, Myers said he went to a neighbor's home and tried to call Williams's attorney, James Harrison.

"I left a message and told him they were bringing 'Boonie' downtown and that we needed him immediately," Myers recalled.[34]

At 3:10 a.m., an officer at the scene approached him and asked, "Didn't you say your name was Nathan Myers?"[35]

"Yes, sir," Myers replied.

"Turn around," the officer said.

"For what?" Myers asked.

"You're under arrest."

He was handcuffed and put in a separate car from his uncle.

Officer Robert Horne described Myers as "scared maybe frightened" as he was placed in the back of his patrol car. When asked to describe what he meant, Officer Horne said, "I can't explain the look, to me he looked like, I'm not saying he was guilty or anything. I'm saying like maybe he was scared like, 'These guys are trying to pin something on me' or, you know, 'I'm going to jail,' just like a worried look just like anybody would be."[36]

Despite their alibis and the supporting statements of others and based solely on Nina Marshall's identification, Clifford Williams and Nathan Myers were arrested at the scene for the murder of Jeanette "Baldie" Williams and the attempted murder of Nina Marshall.

Within hours of their arrest Detective Bowen ordered a gunpowder residue test for both Myers and Williams.[37] The results were: "the amount of antimony found in the hand swabs was insufficient to indicate the presence of gunshot residue: therefore, no testing for barium was conducted. From these findings no conclusion can be drawn as to whether the subject(s) did or did not handle or fire a weapon."[38]

As they were booked into the Duval County jail, Clifford "Boonie" Williams and Nathan Myers had no idea they would not see complete freedom again for almost forty-three years.

5

Pretrial

From the moment of their arrest, Clifford Williams and Nathan Myers proclaimed their innocence. According to Myers, their lawyers agreed.

"They said, 'we will get ya'll out,'" Myers said. "'They ain't got nothing on you, and you got all those witnesses to tell where you were at the time.' They told us not to worry about it, 'you are going to beat this case.'"[1]

Williams and Myers were represented by two well-known private defense attorneys, James Harrison and Ken Vickers. Harrison, a former prosecutor, would eventually be elected as a judge in the Fourth Judicial Circuit and was later appointed general counsel to the City of Jacksonville. Vickers was a highly respected defense attorney with a law degree from Georgetown University. He was regarded by some as one of the better trial lawyers at the time.[2]

The Prosecutor's Office was headed by Ed Austin, a legend in Jacksonville legal and political circles. A former chief public defender, Austin was first elected state attorney in 1969 before he was appointed the city's general counsel in 1972. He returned as state attorney in 1974 and was reelected four times. Austin was elected mayor of Jacksonville in 1991, serving one term.

Ed Austin was a towering, imposing figure with a John Wayne swagger and a folksy southern charm. As state attorney he hired and mentored numerous lawyers who went on to serve in major leadership positions, including another future Jacksonville mayor, John Delaney; a state Supreme Court chief justice, Leander Shaw; and a future president of the Florida Bar, Hank Coxe.

Coxe was a young, charismatic prosecutor, a few years out of law school at Washington and Lee when he was assigned to prosecute the Williams and Myers murder case in the summer of 1976. Coxe had worked his way through college and law school with the merchant marine and found himself in Jacksonville in 1973 while awaiting results of the Florida Bar exam (he had already passed the Virginia Bar). To make ends meet, he worked nights at a warehouse counting automobile parts and spent his afternoons pumping gasoline at a Shell station on St. Johns Avenue. One day, as fate would have it, Ed Austin, who was then the city's general counsel, stopped in to buy gas.[3]

"I think I had just gotten my Florida Bar results a day or two before," Coxe recalled. "He asked me a few questions and then said he was going to put me in touch with Harry Shorstein, who, at the time, was the chief assistant state attorney. All of a sudden, within a few days, I was an assistant state attorney."[4]

For Coxe, it was a "learn as you go" experience. "There was no real training," he said.

He turned to the more experienced prosecutors in the office for advice, saying he had no formal trial training in law school.

"In the beginning, I wasn't even so sure what I was supposed to say in an opening statement."[5]

In his first case as a prosecutor, the jury acquitted the defendant of a misdemeanor in about seven minutes, Coxe recalled. Immediately after the verdict was released, the forewoman went running of out the courtroom.

Coxe asked the court bailiff, "What's with that?" The bailiff responded, "Well, you need to learn to ask questions when you pick a jury. Her husband is on trial for first-degree murder down in Court Room 5."[6]

Among the cases Coxe handled early in his career as a prosecutor was the conviction of Christine Mitchell for selling heroin. At the time of her arrest, Mitchell was having an affair with Clifford Williams. She was sentenced to fifteen years in prison. (Her conviction was subsequently reversed by the District Court of Appeals, which ordered a new trial.)[7] When she was arrested, Mitchell was living in the same Morgan Street apartment that would later be the scene of the deadly shooting on May 2, 1976.

After the Mitchell conviction, Coxe received some unsolicited and unexpected advice from some detectives in the Jacksonville Sheriff's Office.

"We got feedback that you might want to be careful as a result of this case," was the message.

They then handed Coxe a .38 caliber loaded pistol for his protection. It was a stark reminder of the dangers related to the gang and drug scene of the day.[8]

It was Coxe's successful prosecution of Mitchell and his familiarity with some of the key players in the case that most likely resulted in his being appointed prosecutor in the Myers-Williams case.

"There was going to be some overlap in the list of alibi witnesses," Coxe said. "It was the same circle of people."[9]

The judge assigned to the case was Clifford Shepard, a trial judge with a reputation for harsh sentencing who would eventually become chief judge for the Fourth Judicial Circuit. Shepard had also been the presiding judge in the Christine Mitchell case.

Collectively, the individuals assigned to the Myers-Williams case amounted to a literal who's who in the North Florida legal community.

In the two months leading up to the trial there was a flurry of activity, much of which centered around the surviving victim, Nina Marshall, and the possible motive for the shooting and murder.

Three days after the shooting, while she was recovering in the hospital from her injuries, Nina gave a written statement to detectives. Over the course of several interviews and in her trial testimony Marshall's narrative would change considerably with regard to the details of the shooting. But, despite numerous inconsistencies, she never once wavered in her assertion that Clifford Williams and Nathan Myers were the shooters.[10]

Nina's account included statements that she was involved in several activities prior to the shooting on the evening of May 1, including:[11]

- Multiple trips to the Pik-Up-Liquor store
- Listening to records with a friend
- Babysitting and bathing Christine Mitchell's six-year-old child before returning her to her grandmother by 11:15 p.m.

She told authorities that around 11:30 p.m. that evening she rolled four joints of marijuana that she shared in bed with her lover, Jeanette Williams, as they watched television inside the Morgan Street apartment.[12] Nina was on methadone at the time.[13] According to her deposition, Marshall said she was lying on the side of the bed closest to the door, with her legs angled toward the window. Jeanette was on her right side very close to Marshall ("under" her) on the side of the bed closest to the window.[14] Nina recalled watching a late show on the TV, which was sitting on a dresser at the foot of the bed. She dozed off, then awoke at the sound of someone unlocking the apartment door. She thought nothing of it and fell back asleep only to wake up a second time with a burning sensation in her neck from a bullet wound.[15]

When she realized she had been shot, she opened her eyes and saw Williams and Myers standing next to the TV at the foot of the bed. She told police that both were firing handguns that appeared to be wrapped in a blanket or pillows. She said she saw sparks fly from two different directions as both men emptied their guns. Marshall originally told detectives that she lay motionless and played dead until the shooting stopped, allowing her to identify the shooters as Clifford Williams and Nathan Myers as they exited the bedroom into the adjacent living room. According to Marshall's original statement given to police, the two men then left the apartment, locking the deadbolt on the way out. After they left, Marshall said she staggered out of bed, unlocked the front door, and saw Williams and Myers walking west on Morgan Street in the direction of where the party was being held.[16]

Wounded from the shooting, Marshall attempted to get help at a neighbor's apartment, but no one opened the door. A passerby, Harold Torrence, stopped and gave her a ride to University Hospital. She offered little information other than to say she had been shot and that she thought Jeanette was dead. Numerous times he asked who had shot her, but she did not answer. It was only when she was in the hospital emergency room that Marshall identified the shooters as Williams and Myers.[17]

Marshall told police that at no time did she lose consciousness and that "she has no doubt whatsoever as to the identity of the suspects."[18]

She offered police various theories as to a motive for the shooting. The police report made reference to an alleged drug deal that had gone bad between Clifford Williams and the victims the week prior to the shooting. Marshall also said that same week, Clifford threatened her over one hundred dollars of rent money he had put up for her and Jeanette Williams.[19]

"I'm going to show you bull daggers that you're not going to (expletive) over me," Williams threatened, according to Marshall.[20]

During one of her interviews, Marshall told detectives that another possible motive was that Clifford Williams might have been apprehensive that she and Jeanette Williams would report some of his criminal activities to authorities. Both women had been corresponding with Christine Mitchell, Williams's girlfriend, who was serving time for a drug conviction. Mitchell told them, "They should advise Williams that if he did not cease with assaulting her friends that she would tell all that she knew about his business," according to Marshall.[21]

However, in her deposition, Marshall said she couldn't think of any reason that Nathan Myers would have wanted to shoot her or Jeanette.

"No reason whatsoever?" she was asked.[22]

"Nothing but that we heard them talking about some murders and things," she replied.

Marshall alleged a conversation occurred about a month and a half before the shooting and that she heard "they killed a guy and buried him in the woods." Marshall acknowledged being high at the time of the conversation.[23]

Meanwhile, evidence gathered at the scene was proving problematic for Marshall's account of the night's shooting.

The general offense report states, "It should be noted that the physical evidence at the scene is entirely consistent with the statements of the victim."[24]

However, in that same report and in subsequent depositions, the investigating detectives indicate they originally believed the shooting occurred outside and through the window, in sharp contrast to Marshall's account that the shooting took place inside the apartment.[25] The curtains, screen, and window of the north bedroom window all had holes in them. The lower right portion of the window frame "revealed an apparent bullet hole" and had "carbonaceous material" on it.[26]

At his deposition, lead detective Richard Bowen stated, "the physical evidence at the window itself indicated that a projectile of some sort had gone inside of the bedroom from the outside."[27]

Detective J. R. Bradley observed glass fragments on the bed, which he believed to be from the window. The interior of the apartment seemed otherwise undisturbed except for the presence of blood.[28] In reconciling the various discrepancies from how Nina Marshall described the shooting, the detectives concluded, "From physical evidence at the scene, it appears as though the suspects in this case intended to make it look as though the victims had been shot by someone from the bedroom window."[29]

The two-shooter theory was also being shot down by a ballistics report on the bullets and bullet fragments collected at the crime scene. On July 5, 1976, the Tallahassee Regional Criminal Laboratory report concluded that all of the .38 caliber bullets submitted in the case came from a single .38 caliber revolver, including the damaged bullet from Nina Marshall's arm. No other caliber bullets were recovered at the scene, and no other caliber bullets were recovered from the bodies of the victims with the exception of a .32 caliber bullet recovered from the body of Jeanette Williams, which was determined to be from an old, unrelated gunshot wound.[30]

As a trial date approached, two vastly different scenarios emerged.[31] The first was supported by Nina Marshall's eyewitness but inconsistent account that identified Clifford Williams and Nathan Myers as the shooters. Her version was bolstered by the fact that both men were known to have been in the vicinity when the shooting occurred and had keys to her apartment.

As part of the investigation, Detective Bowen noted that the distance between the crime scene and the nearby party where the suspects were seen was "a very short duration." Walking at a medium to fast pace, Bowen said he was able to cover the distance in thirty to thirty-five seconds.[32]

Marshall knew both men well, and there was a history of drug use among them. Clifford Williams was known to Detectives Bradley and Bowen as a drug dealer with an arrest record. Police believed he was dangerous and capable of committing murder. When Nina Marshall identified Williams and Myers as the shooters, police believed they had probable cause to arrest the two men based on the information provided.

The second theory, supported by forensics and physical evidence, had the shooting occurring outside of the apartment, through the bedroom window, by a single gun. This scenario was further supported by multiple witnesses who said Williams and Myers were attending a neighborhood birthday party down the street when the shots were heard. None of the witnesses, including those interviewed by police, recalled seeing either man leave before the shots were fired. Both men, who professed their innocence, were found clean of any gunpowder residue hours after the shooting.

As they awaited their day in court and chance to prove their innocence, Clifford Williams and Nathan Myers were supremely confident.

"We got this," Williams said he was told by his attorneys.[33]

He couldn't have been more wrong.

6

Trial and Error?

The legal system, as it existed back in 1976, was different from the one we know today.

A capital murder case going to trial a little more than two months after an arrest would be highly unlikely in today's environment. According to the Jacksonville State Attorney's Office, present-day homicide cases usually take at least eighteen months or more before going to trial.[1] Sufficient time is needed for forensic analysis, investigation, discovery, and pretrial motions.

Nevertheless, the July 22, 1976, trial date for Clifford Williams and Nathan Myers seemed hastily set even by the standards of the day. Despite the fact that work was being done on the case right up until the trial date, records suggest that the defense attorneys never requested a continuance or delay of the trial. Many of the pleadings, depositions, and forensic reports were dated July 1976.[2] Considering the seriousness of the charges for which the defendants potentially faced the death penalty, such expediency would be unusual in today's courtroom.

It could, however, have been a strategy used by the defense in this particular case, according to then prosecutor Hank Coxe.

"They may have thought Coxe doesn't have it together," he conjectured. "He's got one person who was shot and claims this is what happened. She's impeachable for different reasons . . . and do we want to give Coxe a lot more time to put this together, or is he going to rely on this one witness?"[3]

Williams and Myers were tried together with each retaining his own counsel. Williams was represented by James Harrison and Myers by Ken Vickers, both experienced lawyers.

Despite what appeared to be a significant amount of exculpatory evidence, the attorneys chose not to call any of their own witnesses or put on any evidence on behalf of their clients.

Instead, the defense team opted for a trial strategy of preserving the right to have the last word in front of the jury.[4] In a practice that is no longer allowed, defense attorneys in Florida at one time had an option to present the opening statement and concluding argument to the jury, with the State's closing argument sandwiched in between. But there was a catch. By choosing this "last word" strategy, defense counsel could offer no testimony or call any of their own witnesses except for the defendant, who could testify on their own behalf. Rule 3.250 of the Florida Rules of Criminal Procedure stated: "A defendant offering no testimony in his or her behalf, except the defendant's own, shall be entitled to the concluding argument before the jury."

Deciding on such a strategy was a gamble, requiring attorneys to weigh the impact of speaking to the jury last as opposed to presenting testimony for jury consideration. Long opposed by prosecutors and victim's rights groups, this practice was eventually eliminated from the Florida Rules of Criminal Procedure due in part to the efforts of a Jacksonville legislator, Dick Kravitz. Kravitz had been approached by a constituent who told him she had been raped and that the accused "got away with it" because the defense team used the "last word" strategy.[5] Kravitz became the prime sponsor of a bill in the state legislature that did away with this outdated practice, putting Florida more in line with most states, where prosecutors were given the first and final say before a jury in criminal proceedings. The Florida Supreme Court approved this long-awaited procedural change in 2007.[6]

It was, however, an acceptable practice in 1976 and was utilized by the defense attorneys for Williams and Myers. As the trial proceeded with no defense witnesses or testimony presented, Nathan Myers thought he had been duped.

"They [the lawyers] told us, 'don't worry about it,'" Myers said. "'They ain't got nothing. All they got is this one girl.' I was dumb about the law. When my attorney said they ain't got nothing on us, I believed it. I'm taking his word for it. I paid the man to represent me and he didn't do jack . . . nothing."[7]

The first trial ended in a mistrial when prosecutor Coxe violated the "Golden Rule" that prohibits a lawyer from asking a jury to put themselves in the shoes of a victim, out of a concern that doing so could taint the outcome of a trial.

"Mr. Coxe throwed a mistrial because he knew the case was going our way," Nathan Myers alleged. "He called us cold-blooded murderers right there in front of the jury."[8]

Coxe has a more plausible, if somewhat embarrassing explanation for the mistrial.

"When I did it, I thought it was a brilliant line," Coxe admitted. "It was emotional, persuasive, and it got the jury's attention."[9]

He remembers his statement to the jury:

"I pray to God it never happens to any one of you or anybody in this courtroom, but if [at] any time it should happen, and you are lying in bed with somebody you love, and that person gets murdered, and you get shot twice through the neck and once in the arm, you had better be God-fearing churchgoing Christians the way Mr. Harrison tells it, or you best not come down to the State Attorney's Office or Sheriff's Office and say who did it because you are going to get turned away."[10]

Initially there was no objection from the defense.

"I didn't think there was anything wrong with it, so I did it again about five minutes later," Coxe recalled.[11]

This time, the defense lawyers rose to their feet and called for a mistrial.

"We are up at the bench before Judge Cliff Shepard, and they are yelling that I violated the Golden Rule, and I had no idea what they were talking about," Coxe admitted. "It was hard to come up with a really effective response."[12]

Judge Shepard looked at Coxe incredulously and granted the mistrial.

Coxe went back to his office at the state attorney's headquarters, where he asked some colleagues, "Anybody ever heard of the Golden Rule?"

"Of course, everybody knows the Golden Rule," Coxe said. "Well, you learn, but that's not the way you are supposed to learn."[13]

Following the declaration of a mistrial, Nathan Myers was released briefly on bond. His uncle, a previously convicted felon, remained in prison with no bond offered.

One night during his release, Myers visited the Tip Top bar in downtown Jacksonville.

From his seat near the end of the bar he noticed Nina Marshall enter the lounge. She walked the length of the bar, made eye contact with Myers, and sat down a few seats away from him.

Face-to-face with his accuser, Myers said it took all it could to temper his emotions.[14]

"I was on fire," he said.

He went outside to a nearby phone booth and called his attorney, Ken Vickers.

Myers said Vickers told him to "get away from there. They sent her there to see if you are going to do anything to her. Don't say nothing to her, don't bother with her, just get away from up there."[15]

Myers, who was facing first-degree murder charges, believes he was released on bond because "they wanted to see what my next move was going to be."[16]

A new court date was set for September 1, 1976, with all the same lawyers on both sides and Judge Shepard once again presiding. As the new trial was beginning, Myers said he was summoned to a meeting with prosecutor Coxe.

With his mother seated on one side and his grandmother on the other, Myers said the prosecutor told him, "Myers, today could be your lucky day if you want it to [be]."[17]

Myers said Coxe offered him a plea deal of two years in prison if he would testify against his uncle Clifford Williams. The plea offer was confirmed by Coxe, who recalled the State made an offer of five years in prison.

"My motivation is this kid is just out of high school," said Coxe. "He's a follower of his uncle. He thinks that's a cool world with the drugs, women, guns and all that stuff so I'm thinking why would I not cut him some slack to see if he will cooperate and get up there and tell what we already believed happened."[18]

Myers was having none of it.

"I looked him square in the eye and said, 'No can do,'" Myers recalled. "'I can't do nothing like that.' I said, 'I'm not going to tell no lie on him just to free me.'"[19]

Myers said the prosecutor told him, "You got a lot of guts."

Myers thought it was a "trap."

"My mother and grandmother looked at me and saw the man I was becoming," Myers recalled. "I wasn't going to testify against my uncle. See, that's my blood. He didn't do anything, and I didn't do anything, so why should I lie?"[20]

Years later, after his release from prison, Myers said he harbors no ill will toward Coxe. "I knew he had a job to do," Myers said. "I feel like he was under stress, that Ed Austin put so much pressure on him. He was a couple of years out of law school . . . his hair was all raggedy, his face stayed blush . . . his tie all hanging wild and everything. He looked to me like someone who had been sleeping in his car. He was really burnt-out is how it looked to me."[21]

The second trial proceeded without a plea deal with the same defense lawyers adopting the same "last word" strategy.

The State called six witnesses: Nina Marshall, Officer John Zipperer, Medical Examiner Dr. Peter Lipkovic, Dr. Sam Stephenson (Nina Marshall's surgeon), Detective Richard Bowen, and Harold Torrence, the passerby who transported the wounded Marshall to University Hospital.[22]

The State's case rested primarily on Nina Marshall's eyewitness identification of the shooters.

She testified that she saw Williams and Myers three times during the incident: (1) when she sat up in bed while they were shooting; (2) when she lay on the floor and they stepped over her and looked back at her; and (3) outside the apartment building before she flagged down a ride to the hospital.[23]

Yet she provided inconsistent accounts of her movements during the shooting. In her original written statement to police, she said she lay over Jeanette Williams and played dead until the shooting stopped. However, at the trial, Marshall testified that she sat up and saw the perpetrators. She originally told police she only fell off the bed once, but at the trial she said she fell off three times. She testified that Jeanette grabbed the back of her nightgown as she was falling off the bed and partially onto the top of a nightstand as her neck was bleeding.

However, crime scene photographs show that nothing on top of the nightstand had been disturbed and there were no signs of blood on the table.[24]

There were even inconsistencies in Marshall's account of her activities before the shooting.

For instance, Marshall told police that the child she was babysitting for was watching a "Charlie Brown" special in the living room shortly before she took her home at 11:15 p.m. "Charlie Brown" specials did not air at 11:00 p.m., and a search of the TV Guide showed no "Charlie Brown" special airing on May 1, 1976.[25]

Because of the defense counsel's strategy, the jury was never presented with the physical evidence suggesting the shots came from outside the bedroom window in direct contrast to Marshall's version of the shooting. None of the alibi witnesses were called who could have confirmed Williams and Myers were at a nearby party when the shots were heard. The ballistics evidence indicating that the shots were fired from a single firearm was never introduced. And the jury never heard the results of the negative gunshot residue tests that were conducted on Williams and Myers after the shooting.

Clifford Williams's attorney, James Harrison, only recalled prosecution witness Detective Richard Bowen, who testified that he did not find any evidence of blood on the clothing and shoes he collected from both Williams and Myers.[26] It was Bowen who ordered the swabbing of both defendants' hands for gunshot residue. However, no evidence was presented that the residue tests came back negative.

Attorney Vickers, who represented Myers, waived his opening statement and did not put on any witnesses or evidence to support his client's innocence. Instead, he relied solely on the cross-examination of the State's witnesses to make his case. He zeroed in on Marshall's behavior and her many inconsistencies including:

Marshall's drug use before the shooting.

Inconsistency between her pretrial statements about falling off the bed once and her trial testimony that she fell off the bed three times.

The fact that the nightstand she stated she fell onto was undisturbed and showed no signs of blood.

Her inability to clearly see the shooters' faces based on her testimony that she saw sparks and was dodging bullets.[27]

In his closing argument, Vickers relied on these and other inconsistencies in an attempt to impeach Nina Marshall's credibility as the one and only eyewitness.

The prosecution in its closing argument emphasized the powerful weight of an eyewitness, who in this case was also a victim. "When you have an eyewitness," Coxe told the jury, "you do not need all the forensics, you don't need all that stuff."[28]

The trial took only two days. The jury began deliberations at 8:10 p.m. on September 2 and returned with a verdict less than three hours later, at 10:47 p.m. Clifford Williams and Nathan Myers were both found guilty of first-degree murder and attempted first-degree murder. The State sought the death penalty, but on September 7, the jury rendered an advisory verdict of life in prison for both men.[29] The trial court, however, overrode the jury's recommendation and sentenced Clifford Williams to death and Myers to life.

"This Court cannot conceive of any more heinous, atrocious or cruel act than to enter someone's home in the night while they are sleeping in their bed and shoot them to death," Judge Shepard said.[30]

In sentencing Clifford Williams to death, Judge Shepard said, "This defendant is indeed an extremely dangerous individual who is capable of dealing death to those who oppose him or his illegal schemes in the slightest. . . . The Court concludes that death is the appropriate sentence in this case. . . . May Almighty God have mercy on your soul."[31]

It was a stunning outcome for the two defendants who, despite their questionable and often criminal past, steadfastly maintained their innocence in this case.

Questions would arise over the next many years as to why the attorneys for Williams and Myers did not present the extensive forensic evidence and multitude of alibi witnesses they seemed to have had at their disposal. Both were gifted defense attorneys. Harrison had represented Williams on several other occasions. He told appellate attorney Margaret Good-Earnest, who represented Williams on direct appeal, that Williams had always been truthful with him. When he asked Williams "point blank" if he had anything to do with the shooting, he said he did not.[32] Given his past criminal record, it stood to reason that Williams was not called to testify in his own defense for fear of what might have emerged during cross-examination. Did the same hold true for the alibi witnesses? The neighborhood on Morgan Street was known for its drug and gang activity. Did the defense attorneys worry about the credibility of those witnesses? Was there something else they knew?

Both Harrison and Vickers are deceased, but the issue of their effectiveness as defense counsel would linger as the case would be reexamined nearly four decades later.[33]

And what of Nina Marshall, also now deceased? What was her motive for specifically identifying Williams and Myers as the shooters? Bleeding from her gunshot wounds in a hospital emergency room, what reason could she possibly have to accuse Myers and Williams if she wasn't positive?

And while her pretrial statements and testimony were often inconsistent, she never once deviated from her claim that Myers and Williams were the shooters.

"A theory is that one of them owed Boonie some money and he jumped on them," Myers recalled. "Maybe she was jealous of my relationship with Baldie, who was her lover. We [Myers and Baldie] had a brother-sister relationship."[34]

Clifford Williams acknowledged that he and Marshall had a dispute in the weeks prior to the shooting. "She messed up some of my drugs," he said. But he recalled they had gone to dinner the night before the shooting and patched things up.[35]

In the final analysis, the defense strategy of not presenting evidence or witnesses in order to have the "last word" before the jury proved to be ineffective. As a result, the jury was left only with Marshall's eyewitness (albeit inconsistent) account of the shooting.

Eyewitness testimony has long been considered among the most convincing forms of evidence in criminal trials.[36] Yet research has shown that eyewitness identification is vulnerable and not always reliable. A study by the Innocence Project reported that 71 percent of death sentence exonerees who had been cleared by DNA had been convicted through eyewitness misidentification.[37] Given the trauma of the shooting, Marshall's relationship with the accused, and her drug use, her eyewitness account would be subject to scrutiny in the years following the conviction.

As Clifford Williams headed to death row and eighteen-year-old Nathan Myers was beginning his life sentence there were many unanswered questions. The four months since the shooting on Morgan Street had produced a buzz of activity and legal maneuvers in what may have appeared as just another capital murder case in Jacksonville, Florida.

But in many ways, this story was only beginning.

7

Invest in a Vest

Police Officer John Zipperer was on his early-morning patrol beat on August 30, 1976, when he heard a radio dispatch about a possible burglary at the Rib Crib restaurant on Davis Street. It had already been an active few months for the rookie patrolman. He was the first officer on the scene at the murder of Jeanette "Baldie" Williams and was preparing to testify in two days on behalf of the State at the second trial of Clifford Williams and Nathan Myers.

As had become his recent practice, Zipperer was wearing his bulletproof vest, which was something new for Jacksonville police officers. The vests were made possible by a privately funded community initiative known as "Invest in a Vest" sparked by the death of a young patrol officer in 1975.[1]

The original vests were heavy and hot.

"A lot of the guys didn't wear them because they weren't mandated," Zipperer recalled. "But I always felt this lady who provided them cared enough about us to do this, we ought to care enough to wear them."[2]

It turned out to be a lifesaving decision.

After he investigated the scene at the Rib Crib restaurant and determined the building was secure, Zipperer went looking for potential suspects. At the corner of Fourth and Davis Streets, he noticed a pedestrian walking alone. The time was about 3:00 a.m. Zipperer pulled up to the curb and called out, "Hey partner, hold on, let me talk to you for a minute."[3]

As he exited his patrol car, he realized he had left his patrolman's cap in his car. It was police policy that if you were outside of your car, you had to be wearing your cap.

"About a week or so before, I had gotten chewed out for being out of my car without my hat on," Zipperer said.[4]

As he was putting on his cap, the suspect pulled a gun. Zipperer responded by saying, "Look, buddy, you don't want to do that." The suspect fired five shots, two of which hit Zipperer in the chest and were deflected by the bulletproof vest. The young officer returned the fire, hitting the suspect three times below the waist.[5]

Stunned and out of breath from the impact of the bullets hitting his vest, Zipperer staggered back into his patrol car to radio for help. Given the pain he was experiencing, he wasn't so sure the vest had even worked. The suspect lay wounded on the sidewalk and began reaching for his gun. Dizzy and in pain, Zipperer managed to kick the gun out of the way before passing out on top of the suspect. Two other police officers who had responded to the same burglary call at the Rib Crib heard the nearby shots and arrived at the scene in time to take charge.

Zipperer was taken to a hospital, where he was treated for bruises and released. The vest had clearly saved his life. As it turned out, the wounded suspect was an escaped prisoner from Louisiana, where he was serving a one-hundred-year sentence for a shooting in New Orleans.

Zipperer said he shot the escapee in the leg and groin. "They took four inches of bone in his right leg and he can't make any more babies. That wasn't intentional; I was just slinging lead."[6]

Zipperer's heroics and the bulletproof vest were featured in the Jacksonville newspaper, and he was presented a key to the city of New Orleans for his role in the recapture of the escapee.

"I just happened to run into him," he said of the encounter.[7]

Zipperer was able take the stand two days after the shooting to testify for the prosecution in the case against Clifford Williams and Nathan Myers. Prosecutor Hank Coxe recalled the injured Zipperer could hardly walk the day of his testimony.[8]

Despite the lack of evidence to support it, there were bound to be questions as to the timing and circumstances surrounding Zipperer's shooting. Was it simply coincidental, or had he been set up two days before he was to take the stand in the Myers-Williams murder case?

According to Zipperer, Lonnie Miller, a detective with the Jacksonville Sheriff's Office Intelligence Unit, had his own opinion. "He told us it was a hit put out by 'Boonie,'" Zipperer said.[9]

Detective Lonnie Miller was a highly regarded twenty-five-year veteran of the Jacksonville police force known for his extensive work with children in the Black community. He was shot and killed while assisting another officer with a robbery call in May 1996. A 100-plus-acre regional park in Northwest Jacksonville is named in his honor.[10]

More than forty-four years after the incident, Zipperer says he has no evidence or proof that his shooting was a setup. "I was a rookie cop, and Lonnie Miller had been around forever, so a lot of people believed whatever he said. There was never any follow-up or investigation. Since 'Boonie' already got life, what else were you going to do to him?"[11]

While Zipperer has no reason to believe he was set up, he does harbor strong opinions about the Conviction Integrity Review (CIR) unit that would ultimately exonerate Clifford Williams and Nathan Myers.

Zipperer, a forty-five-year veteran of law enforcement, is a harsh critic of the review of the case and made his thoughts known inside the State Attorney's Office, where he was working as an investigator before his official retirement in June 2020.

"It was my belief that what they were doing was wrong," Zipperer said. "These two individuals were given a fair trial. They were represented by, at the time, good defense attorneys. They were prosecuted by a good state attorney, Hank Coxe. There was no lying or cheating. Everything was straight-up. Hank presented the case, and the jury found them guilty. For you to come back forty-five years later and say they are not guilty is totally wrong. You cannot prove these fellas are not guilty. You may not be able to prove they are guilty again, but you already proved it."[12]

There would be much more to say about that very issue in the four and a half decades after the conviction of Nathan Myers and Clifford Williams.

8

Fat Time

"Anything that's on the outside you can get on the inside except a car and a real woman," said Nathan Myers of his years in the Florida prison system. "It's drug infested, and the cops are crooked as hell."[1]

That is only part of his perspective. During his nearly forty-three years of incarceration, Myers missed most of his adult life. He also lost his entire nuclear family: his mother, father, grandmother, and sister. He was unable to attend family funerals or even say goodbye. He reflected that there is no way to fully comprehend the passage of time for him or his uncle Clifford "Boonie" Williams.[2]

Each man spent more than fifteen thousand days in prison, a time span covering the terms of eight United States presidents.

Williams spent the first four years of his sentence on Florida's death row. The jury had recommended life for both him and his nephew Nathan. However, Judge Clifford Shepard overrode the jury's recommendation and sentenced Williams, a previously convicted felon, to death.

Both men filed direct appeals. Ultimately, the Florida Supreme Court, in a 4–3 ruling, said there were no aggravating factors to support the death penalty and reversed Williams's sentence to life. Nathan Myers's life sentence was affirmed and upheld on appeal.

"When I first went to prison, I knew I had to stand up to be a man," Myers said. "The most important thing is that you've got to stand up and protect yourself and keep yourself safe. I had a motto, 'Kill or be killed.'"[3]

Florida has the nation's third-largest prison system. It's been the subject of numerous investigations by journalists, advocacy groups, and government agencies. Some have revealed a culture of corruption and abuse and even death. Many of the prisons are located deep in the heart of Florida's most rural counties, insulated from the general public, who have minimal awareness of what goes on behind the prison walls.[4]

Myers's description of life inside the Florida prison system rings all too familiar:

"You had guys that would rob you. Guys that would try to turn you out to be homosexual. You have to deal with the officers and their crap. They don't care nothing about you. They don't care if you get busted in the head with a lock or stuck with a knife. They just want to keep you from going across that fence."[5]

Early on, Myers said he was put to the test by prison guards at the Sumter Correctional Institution. He had just returned from a prison work shift and was preparing to watch an afternoon episode of the soap opera *General Hospital,* which had become his custom. As he passed his cell, he noticed some prison officers on his bed going through his property. When he asked what was happening, one of the guards replied, "You come with us."[6]

He was then escorted to a small room he said was known as the "Goon Squad" office. Once inside, an officer covered up the peep hole that allowed someone on the outside to peek in. It was just Myers alone with four prison guards. Three were white; one was Black.

"The Black officer looked to me like he wanted to be in charge, so he grabbed a chair and told me to sit down," Myers recalled. "I told him that was the oldest trick in the game," wary that if he tried to sit, the other officers would kick the chair out from under him to get him on the ground. When he refused, the Black officer began circling around him. Myers said he followed suit and began circling around the officer.[7]

"Oh, you want to be tough, you want to be bad?" the officer asked. A struggle ensued, and Myers was pinned to the wall with the other officers ready to rush him. By chance, Myers's work supervisor passed by the office and heard the pounding. When he demanded entry, the door was opened, and Myers avoided what was likely to have been a physical beating.

"They tried to jump me," Myers explained. A complaint was filed, and the Black officer was suspended for thirty days. "They wanted me to be afraid of them, but I wasn't going to be intimidated."[8]

Myers said it was a constant battle, whether dealing with other inmates or prison officers. He had fights with both. "If you get into any trouble, you're on your own."[9]

And, over the span of forty-three years and nine different prison facilities, there was plenty of trouble.

When he first entered prison at the Sumter Correctional Institution, Myers said he was still living the "bad life . . . smoking pot, gambling." All the vices he relied on outside of prison were readily available on the inside, and he was hustling. "There was nothing you couldn't get for a price."[10]

Prison life required you establish an identity, and the streetwise Myers initially played the game, bribing cops for drugs and turning money any way he could.

He earned his prison nickname "Fat Time" in January 1978. He and five other inmates were watching Super Bowl XII between the Denver Broncos and the Dallas Cowboys.

"We went and bought us some weed," Myers recalled. "I stuck some papers together and rolled a big, long fat joint." As they passed it around and inhaled, one of the inmates remarked, "Hey I got a new name for you," referring to Myers. "Party Time with Fat Time." From that day until the day he left prison, Myers was known as "Fat Time."[11]

Everyone had a nickname. "The only time you ever use your real name is when they come by at night to make sure you are in the right bunk," Myers said.[12]

During his sentence, "Fat Time" served time in nine different Florida prisons, some more than once:

Sumter Correctional Institution; Baker Correctional Institution; Columbia Correctional Institution; Cross City Correctional Institution; Charlotte Correctional Institution; Hamilton Correctional Institution; Okeechobee Correctional Institution; Union Correctional Institution; and the Northwest Florida Reception Center in Washington County.

Some of the transfers were based on Myers's desire to be closer to his family in Jacksonville. At no time was he at the same prison as his uncle Clifford. An effort was made to ensure they were kept apart, Myers said. They would occasionally see each other at a weekend prison softball game when one prison team would travel to another facility for the competition. For Myers, the softball games were a welcome relief from the darkness of prison life.

While the various prisons were different, the system for obtaining drugs and other contraband at them was often similar. All the prisons offered ample opportunities for drugs.

"First, you find you a crooked cop," Myers said. "He can trust you and you can trust him, and you can make your deal. If he likes it, he'll go for it."[13]

Clifford Williams, who worked the same "system" during his prison stay, said identifying prison officers who would supply the drugs was easy. "They find you," he said.[14]

Myers said prison guards who were on the take were always looking for money. "A lot of them were broke," he said. Myers would use cash sent to him by his family to pay off the guards. "Dirty uses," he called it.

The usual method to secure the dope was for the guards to do the dirty work during a shakedown of the prison cell.

"They wouldn't tell you what day they would bring it but they'd come by and shake your house down and leave it [the drugs] there," Myers said. "When people see them shake your house down, they haul tail because they don't want their house shook down next. So, the cop would leave it for you somewhere like your locker and then say, 'They ain't nothing here so let's go.' But you'd sit back and go back in your house and get your dope they left."[15]

According to Myers, anything on the street was available in prison. "Pills, heroin, cocaine, pot, mollies," he said. "All the drugs you want were in prison."[16]

The culture of the street was easily transitioned into prison life. Just like on the outside there were good cops and bad cops, according to Myers. Sometimes the prisoners were used by the good cops to set up the bad ones. "They needed the inmates' help," Myers said. "If a good cop could bust a bad one who was dealing drugs, he'd move up in rank."[17]

Gambling was another facet of daily prison life. They played "skins" and shot dice, according to Myers. On occasion the cops would join in. "I had one cop who gambled cards with me in Okeechobee, and he was a damn captain," Myers said. "He gave me cigarettes to sell for him."[18]

Despite the gambling games and pot parties, prison life was no holiday. Fights were constant, the atmosphere permeated by fear and intimidation. Myers recalled more than one instance where a prisoner was found dead in his cell with the cause of death uncertain. Living conditions on the inside were often deplorable due to poor maintenance and upkeep.

All the while maintaining his innocence of the Morgan Street shootings, Myers was convinced he was being punished for his past behavior and bad choices. "I might have gotten away with things that I should not have gotten away with, and this is how God was punishing me," he reasoned.[19]

It was a notion scoffed at by his mother, who scolded him for such thoughts. "God doesn't punish people like that," she told him. "God only punishes you for what you did."[20]

To face the despair, Myers said it was his observation that a person with a prison sentence will do everything he can to survive and to make it as comfortable as possible. If it takes buying and selling drugs to do it, he will. Myers considers himself to be one of the lucky ones because of his family support. In addition to the regular visits from his mother and sister, he had other relatives and friends who supported him and believed in his innocence. Some would send him money, which he would use to improve his status and standard of living on the inside. "If I had someone who sent me thirty dollars, I'd turn it to make some more." Sometimes the extra money went to the prison laundry. Myers liked to dress sharp, and, like everything else, getting your pants creased came with a price.[21]

Sometimes he used the money to bribe officers to free a fellow inmate from being held in an isolated holding cell, a kind of prison bail bondsman.

It was hardly an environment that fostered rehabilitation. "You can't get better unless you take it upon yourself to get away from that stuff, all the hustlers and the guys doing bad things. You go to church; you don't mess with those things. If they see you go to church, the bad guys don't want to be around you."[22]

While in prison Myers would ultimately rediscover his religious roots. Ironically, he would also find the love of his life, which saved him from self-destruction and set him on a journey of personal transformation on the way to establishing his innocence of a murder charge.

And, in the halls of the Sumter Correctional Institution, he would also reconnect with a childhood friend who would ultimately open a door to his freedom.

9

Salvation

"Oh boy, thank God, I don't know where I'd be without Rose," Nathan Myers reflected.[1]

Quite possibly he might still be in prison. While he and his uncle Clifford steadfastly maintained their innocence, there was little interest in their case and seemingly no chance of having their life sentences overturned. Despite what they felt was inadequate and ineffective representation at their trial, the path to a new hearing seemed out of reach. Both men filed motions alleging they only learned about the physical evidence that the shootings came from the bedroom window and the exculpatory ballistics evidence pointing to a single gun upon filing a public records request.[2] Appeals were denied or never heard. They had no advocates, no private lawyers, and no hope.

Meanwhile, Nathan and Clifford found themselves meshing right into the dark side of prison life, much as they had done on the streets of Jacksonville. Dope was readily attainable, and the survival mentality of gang life translated well behind bars.

"A lot of what I did in prison, the bad things, was to cope with my situation," Myers admitted.

"I was always looking for something."[3]

Initially, Myers became a Muslim. For almost half of his time in prison, he studied Islam and read the Koran with the help of a fellow inmate.

"I was reaching out, trying to find some help," Myers said. "Eventually, I saw some things that didn't fit in Islam, so I made a vow to go back to my faith."[4]

Myers had been raised as a Christian, going to church every Sunday morning, even though the Saturday night before he most likely had been out on the street hustling and smoking dope, hardly the epitome of a Christian life. However, something about those Sundays in church would eventually resonate with him.

His sister, who was an evangelist, pressured Nathan to return to his Christian roots while he was in prison.

"If you don't accept Jesus Christ as your savior, you will never be set free," she told him repeatedly.[5]

If Myers needed someone to help guide his journey to turn his life around, he found it in a Jacksonville cosmetologist seven years his senior.

Rose Denard was in cosmetology school trying to make ends meet while raising a five-year-old daughter. She spent much of her free time visiting her husband, who was serving a prison sentence at the Union Correctional Institution in Raiford, Florida. With its infamous main housing facility, better known as "The Rock," it was among the most notorious of Florida's prisons where the worst of the worst were housed to serve hard time under hard conditions. Some of its more notable inmates included serial killers Ted Bundy and Danny Rolling, also known as the "Gainesville Ripper." Rose's husband was in for robbery and kidnapping.

Visitors would congregate across the street from the prison, often in the early hours of the morning, to sign in and present themselves to the prison authorities. After a while, the visitors got to know one another.

"People would come from all over to visit their loved ones, and we became like a little family," Rose recalled. It was there, in 1981, that she first met Nathan's mother, Dot, who was visiting her son, who had recently been transferred to Raiford. "We soon became the best of friends."[6]

At first Rose took little notice and had no real interest in Nathan, given that she was still married. The only thing she noticed is that he walked with a confident but awkward-looking strut that she found to be funny. Other than that, there was no interest on her part. For Nathan it was a different story—love at first sight.

"I saw a beautiful woman. I saw her as my flavor. I saw the way she acted. The way she talked. I never saw her where she didn't seem happy where she was at. You know when you see a woman walking down the street that you like or would like to hit on . . . well that's what it was."[7]

Nathan also took a liking to Rose's five-year-old daughter. The prison had a play area for visiting children known as the Kiddie Corner. Nathan would interact with the little girl, even teaching her how to write her name.

He was cautious at first. "I wasn't flirting with her [Rose] because I didn't want to cause no problem between her and her husband."[8]

While Rose seemed oblivious to Nathan's interests, her inmate husband was suspicious.

"He's always watching you," he told her. He eventually threatened her if anything ever came of it.[9]

Once, after Nathan had been in confinement for some prison misbehavior, he called his mother to ask if she had been in touch with Rose. "I talk to her all the time," was the reply. "Do you know she's fixin' to get a divorce?"[10]

"Well, check this out," Nathan said when hearing the news. He told his mother to ask Rose if it would be OK for him to write her. "She said 'yes,' and we've been kicking it ever since."[11]

They corresponded by mail on a regular basis beginning in 1984 as her divorce was being finalized. When her soon to be ex-husband found out the two were corresponding, his threats intensified. "One of these days you are going to look up and see me and they are going to shoot me off the fence," he told her.[12]

The correspondence and visits continued. After her divorce, Nathan asked Rose to marry him. She resisted. He was seven years younger than her and facing life in prison.

"One day, if you get out, you'll see a younger woman and you'll go for her," she told him.[13]

Her pastor agreed that marriage was not a good idea. "You shouldn't marry anyone incarcerated with a life sentence," he told her.[14]

When Myers was transferred to the Washington County prison in the Florida Panhandle, they went five years without seeing one another. The drive from Jacksonville was too far for Rose.

When he was transferred back to Baker County, closer to Jacksonville, Rose went to visit him the very first weekend. "I had really missed him," she recalled. Their courtship continued through more than a decade of prison transfers and uncertainty.[15]

Nathan and Rose eventually married in November 2005, a little more than twenty-nine years since he first entered prison. The process of getting to the altar was itself a study of prison bureaucracy.

"First I had to go to the chaplain, the chaplain had to go to the warden, the warden had to write a letter to Tallahassee," Myers said, clicking them off like a checklist. "Then I had to go see a psychologist to see if my mind was OK. All the tests came back that I can get married."[16]

The next challenge was finding a preacher. Because he was still practicing Islam, the prison preacher, who was Christian, said he couldn't conduct the ceremony. Nathan's sister couldn't perform the ceremony either but found someone who could. They were married inside the prison chapel, Rose dressed in pink and black and Nathan in his prison blues.

"That's where married life began, right there in the Baker County jail," said Nathan.[17]

Change did not come easy for Nathan, but his relationship with Rose was giving him some sense of purpose beyond prison life. Even during their prison courtship, he was still hustling, smoking pot, and living a life that, in part, landed him in prison in the first place, even though he maintained his innocence of the murder charge. Any chance of parole was offset by his prison behavior and an accumulation of disciplinary reports.

Over time, Myers began to change his ways.

"If I would have just sat back and let the time do me, I'd still be sitting in prison today," Myers reflected.[18]

He stopped smoking pot in 2000 and stopped gambling in 2002. He enrolled in prison rehab and vocational programs and went on to become a facilitator for other prisoners.

Most important, he said, was the choice he made to be with God. He returned to his Christian faith and became a regular at Sunday church services.

"I didn't want any more of that other life," Myers said. "I wanted my freedom. I didn't want to die in prison. The only way I could get out was to get on my knees, skin 'em up, pray, and keep fighting. And that's what I did."[19]

He also turned his attention away from hustling and toward getting his case reheard in court.

He was a grown man now, determined and focused on his faith, Rose, and his freedom.

In 2013, Myers had a hearing before the parole board. Feeling that he'd turned his life around, Myers entered the meeting hopeful. Despite having received numerous recommendations and commendations, parole was denied. To his further disappointment, he was told his next hearing would not take place until 2020.

"Seven more years?" Myers recalled was his reaction. "You're telling me that no matter what I do it's going to be seven more years before I see you again? No can do."[20]

He redoubled his efforts to work on his case.

For legal advice, Nathan turned to an old friend and a fellow inmate, Tony Brown. Born in 1957, Tony had grown up with Nathan in the Blodgett

Homes project in Jacksonville. They occasionally attended the same schools and hung out regularly in the neighborhood.

As adults, their lives continued to intertwine, mostly in prison. Brown served three different prison sentences: 1974–79; 1980–93; and 1994–2023.[21] He was doing time for robbery in 1976 when he met up with his childhood friend Nathan, who had just been sent to the same Sumter Correctional Institution shortly after his murder conviction. They would meet up again at Raiford in the 1980s and for a third time when both returned to Sumter County.

Myers looked to Brown as his "jailhouse lawyer."

"He knew the law," Myers said. "He was so good because all he did was spend time studying the law in the prison library. I called him my lawyer."

Myers said Brown worked up paperwork for him to file several appeals. In 1987, Myers filed a motion for postconviction relief, claiming his counsel was ineffective for (1) failing to call forty-four alibi witnesses who would have testified that he was at a nearby party during the time of the shooting; (2) failing to allow Myers to testify in his own defense; and (3) failing to call an expert witness to discuss the effects of methadone on a heroin addict [the victim Nina Marshall].

The motion was summarily denied two months after it was filed.[22]

Frustrated but patient, Myers asked the court in 2013 about the status of one of his earlier appeals. A year later he was informed the appeal had been denied back in 1980.

In 2014, Myers filed a *pro se* amended motion for postconviction relief that was contested by the State and summarily denied.[23]

Despite these setbacks, Tony Brown was still to play a pivotal role in the exoneration of Nathan Myers and Clifford Williams in ways that no one could have imagined.

10

Confession

Tony Brown, a habitual offender and Nathan Myers's childhood friend, had recently been released from prison and had just gotten off work at the Dinsmore Work Release Center when he wandered over to Deuce's nightclub on Pearl Street in downtown Jacksonville. It was around April 1993, to the best of Brown's recollection.[1]

While in the Deuce's parking lot he was approached by an old acquaintance, Nathaniel Lawson, a known street thug with a dangerous reputation. According to Brown, Lawson liked to brag about shooting people and ran around with a heroin dealer nicknamed "Cryin' Shame."[2]

On this particular night, Brown and Lawson began exchanging stories of "the old days in the projects" and comparing their criminal misdeeds, of which there were many. At one point, Lawson offered a startling revelation. He told Brown that Clifford "Boonie" Williams and Nathan Myers were serving time for a shooting that he had committed. He said he was paid by Albert Young, a known heroin dealer from the Blodgett Homes project, to shoot Jeanette Williams because she owed him money for some heroin that her lover, Nina Marshall, had stolen from him. (Albert Young was murdered in the 1980s.)[3]

Nathaniel Lawson told Tony Brown that he went to the apartment at 1550 Morgan Street and began peeking in the bedroom window, looking for Jeanette Williams and saw her lying in bed. He said he started shooting from outside the bedroom window and killed Jeanette Williams and shot Nina Marshall, trying to kill her as well. After the shooting, he ran, jumped across the fence in the back of the apartment, and ran to a car driven by Rico Rivers, who was parked waiting for him on Beaver Street. He said Rivers drove him to the Hilltop apartments, where they stayed until the next day.[4]

"I didn't know if he was lying or bragging or trying to impress me," Tony

Brown said, "because I never questioned why he was telling this to me and I didn't care."[5]

Initially, Tony Brown told no one about Nathaniel Lawson's confession. Knowing Lawson's reputation for violence, he didn't want to endanger his own life. As it turned out, Tony Brown wasn't the only person to whom Lawson allegedly confessed.

Leatrice Carter and her husband owned a beer-and-wine tavern near the corner of Jefferson and Beaver Streets in downtown Jacksonville. She remembers Nathaniel Lawson coming into the tavern sometime in the early 1990s. She knew Lawson from having grown up in the Black Bottom neighborhood in Northwest Jacksonville.[6] It was a tight-knit neighborhood. Lawson, Clifford Williams, and Leatrice's brother, Eddie Lee Rosemond, all grew up together. Each would have an extensive rap sheet.

When Lawson arrived at the tavern, he pulled up his shirt, revealing a long, silver gun. "You won't be needing that here," she told him. Lawson went on to tell Leatrice that "Boonie" Williams was in prison for nothing. He admitted to the murder of Jeanette Williams and said that "no one was mad at him except Dot and Frank."[7] Dot was Clifford Williams's sister and Nathan Myers's mother. Frank was Clifford Williams's brother.

Lawson said nothing else to Leatrice about the shooting, and she didn't ask to know more. Leatrice had been close to Clifford Williams and knew that he and his nephew Nathan were in prison for the 1976 murder. Leatrice did tell Ron Stansell, a childhood friend of Nathan Myers, about her conversation with Lawson but no one else.[8] (Leatrice Carter would marry Clifford Williams shortly after his release from prison.)

From the moment of their arrest, Dot Myers was convinced that her son Nathan and brother Clifford were not involved in the shooting of Jeanette Williams and Nina Marshall. She spent years knocking on doors and conducting her own investigation of the incident.[9] Word on the street was that someone else had done the shooting from outside the apartment, not inside as Nina Marshall had alleged.

Dot's brother Frank Williams had heard rumors that Nathaniel Lawson might have somehow been involved in the shooting. Frank at one time had dated Lawson's sister Diane. When he confronted Lawson for the first time near a bar off Jefferson Street, Lawson told Frank he was "staying out of it" and refused to speak with him further.[10]

Sometime later, Diane told Frank that her brother was sick and might want to clear his conscience. Through her husband she helped arrange a meeting.

The two men met in public across the street from the Dayspring Baptist Church in downtown Jacksonville. There, Lawson confessed to Frank Williams that he was the shooter.

"She was stealing from me and I had to send a message," Lawson said.[11] This version differs from his alleged confession to Tony Brown in which he said he was paid to do the shooting.

Frank told Lawson he had ruined the lives of his brother and nephew by having them spend their lives in prison for a crime he had committed. Lawson replied there was nothing more he could do but send them money, which he said he did through Dot.[12]

Dot later acknowledged to her brother that Lawson had indeed sent her some money, which she then passed on to her son Nathan and brother Clifford in prison.[13]

Frank Williams had been a forty-two-year employee of Maxwell House Coffee before he retired.[14] He was aware of his brother "Boonie's" reputation and police record. He had not been at the neighborhood party on Morgan Street, but his brother told him he had nothing to do with the shooting.[15]

Frank was pressured by the family to go to the authorities with the Lawson confession. "It was my word against Nathaniel Lawson's word," Frank said. "The people downtown already convicted my brother; they weren't going to do anything with that." He had hoped Lawson would go to the authorities on his own, but it never happened. Williams said he contacted an attorney to look into the case but was told nothing could be done.[16]

In addition to Tony Brown, Leatrice Carter, and Frank Williams, there would be at least one other person to whom Nathaniel Lawson would allegedly confess. James Stepps was a longtime friend of Lawson. The two had grown up together and stayed close throughout the years right up until Nathaniel Lawson's death in 1994. Stepps sang at Lawson's funeral.[17]

Shortly before he died, Lawson received a visit from Stepps at his apartment off Moncrief Road.

They had some drinks, and Lawson mentioned he wanted to send some money to "Boonie" Williams. He told Stepps he was responsible for killing the woman that Boonie had been sent to prison for. "What can I do?" Lawson asked. "I can't turn myself in."

Because he felt his friend had told him this in confidence, Stepps did not come forward at the time.[18]

For whatever reason, no one to whom Nathaniel Lawson confessed went to law enforcement after hearing his story. Given his reputation for violence, perhaps they feared some type of retribution. As the street code goes, "snitches end up in ditches." Maybe they thought Lawson's story was simply bravado. It would be decades before those to whom Lawson allegedly confessed would speak to authorities.

Meanwhile, Myers and Williams were languishing in jail. Appeals from both were leading nowhere. Over the course of the decades they spent in prison, many of their alibi witnesses died. So had many of their friends and family members. And perhaps most importantly, so had Nathaniel Lawson.

Tony Brown kept the secret of Lawson's confession to himself until he entered Sumter Correctional Institution and once again came across his friend Nathan Myers in 2014. He told Myers of the 1993 meeting with Lawson and what Lawson had said. Myers asked Brown if he would be willing to sign a sworn affidavit.[19] Brown agreed and signed the sworn statement detailing Lawson's confession on October 21, 2014, more than twenty-one years after hearing the confession and more than thirty-eight years after the murder of Jeanette "Baldie" Williams.

After the affidavit, Myers began a flurry of court filings, all of which were denied. After so many years it seemed doubtful that anyone would listen.

But in Jacksonville's Fourth Judicial Circuit, change was afoot in the State Attorney's Office that would turn this decades-old case on its head.

11

Lightning Strikes

Angela Corey was a lightning rod.

The granddaughter of Syrian immigrants, the veteran prosecutor was the first woman to hold the position of state attorney for Florida's Fourth Judicial Circuit, which includes Jacksonville and the surrounding counties of Clay and Nassau.

Throughout much of her thirty-five-year career as a distinguished prosecutor, Corey attracted controversy.

She was first hired by State Attorney Ed Austin in 1981. She remained in the Prosecutor's Office after Austin's successor, Harry Shorstein, was appointed by Governor Lawton Chiles to fill the position when Austin was elected mayor of Jacksonville. As an assistant state attorney, she successfully prosecuted several hundred cases, including numerous homicides. She served in a variety of leadership roles, which included supervising and helping train lawyers in the State Attorney's Office.

Over time, her working relationship with Shorstein was strained. In 2006 she announced her intention to run for state attorney. Shorstein subsequently fired Corey, citing "long-term issues" relating to her supervisory performance.[1] Corey was then hired by John Tanner, state attorney for the neighboring Seventh Judicial Circuit.

In February 2007, Shorstein announced he would not seek reelection as state attorney and threw his support to his chief assistant, Jay Plotkin. Corey defeated Plotkin handily in the 2008 election.

Known to be as combative in public as she was in the courtroom, Corey wasted little time cleaning house. She fired half of the office's investigators, two-fifths of its victim's advocates, a quarter of its thirty-five paralegals and forty-eight support staff, more than one-fifth of the office.[2]

She then penned a letter to Florida senators demanding that they oppose Shorstein's potential nomination as a US attorney, saying, "he should not hold a position of authority in his community again because of his penchant for using the grand jury for personal vendettas."[3]

Shorstein did not receive the appointment and returned to private practice.

As state attorney, Corey presided over several highly publicized cases. In 2011, her office oversaw the case of twelve-year-old Cristian Fernandez, who was charged with killing his two-year-old half brother. Corey maintained that the juvenile system was not equipped to handle cases as serious as murder, so Fernandez was charged as an adult with first-degree murder and aggravated child abuse. Despite stating that her office would not seek a life sentence for Fernandez, Corey's decision to charge him as an adult received considerable negative coverage. He was the youngest person ever to be charged with first-degree murder in Jacksonville.

A team of high-profile attorneys rushed to represent Fernandez, pro bono.

Among them was Hank Coxe, the former prosecutor in the Myers-Williams case, who had become one of the city's best-known defense attorneys. Joining Coxe was veteran attorney Buddy Schulz of Holland & Knight and a lesser-known Melissa Nelson, described as a "star" in the international firm of McGuireWoods. After a series of negotiations, Fernandez pled guilty as a juvenile to manslaughter and aggravated battery.[4]

Corey's highest-profile case occurred when she was appointed by Florida governor Rick Scott as special prosecutor to investigate the killing of Trayvon Martin by George Zimmerman. Zimmerman was the neighborhood watch volunteer who shot and killed the unarmed seventeen-year-old Martin on February 26, 2012. The Sanford County police department determined there was no probable cause to arrest Zimmerman, who claimed he acted in self-defense. That decision sparked protests and nationwide outrage over racial profiling and Florida's controversial "Stand Your Ground" law.

Following her investigation, Corey filed second-degree murder charges against Zimmerman in an affidavit that was sharply criticized by well-known and controversial Harvard attorney Alan Dershowitz, who was part of the O. J. Simpson defense team. Dershowitz maintained the affidavit was misleading and too weak to support the second-degree murder charge. The affidavit, however, was upheld, and Zimmerman stood trial in Seminole

County. On July 13, 2013, the six-women jury panel acquitted Zimmerman of second-degree murder and the lesser included offense of manslaughter.

The verdict and Corey's conduct during the trial drew sharp public rebuke. Dershowitz said she should be disbarred.

"She was among the most irresponsible prosecutors I've seen in 50 years of litigating," Dershowitz said in a highly publicized interview with conservative political commentator Mike Huckabee. "She, by the way, has a horrible reputation in Florida. She's known for overcharging; she's known for being highly political. And, in this case of course, she overcharged."[5]

Dershowitz wasn't alone. Dan Markel, D'Alemberte Professor of Law at Florida State University, said from the moment he reviewed evidence regarding the Zimmerman case online, he thought a charge of second-degree murder was inappropriate.

"In light of the physical evidence and eyewitness testimony statements, it seemed there would be almost no plausible way for the state to surmount the burden of proof, which requires the state to show beyond a reasonable doubt that Zimmerman did not act in self-defense," Markel told *thegrio*, a Black American news outlet.[6]

In addition, there were accusations by her former information technology chief that she violated the rules of discovery by withholding evidence from Zimmerman's defense team. The employee was dismissed.[7]

Corey became a target of the *Florida Times-Union* newspaper in Jacksonville, which ran numerous articles and editorials critical of her performance as state attorney. She refused to speak with the newspaper for a year. Her numerous accomplishments as state attorney were often overshadowed by the negative publicity she generated. As she faced reelection in 2016 for another term as state attorney, Corey was carrying a lot of political baggage and a lot of unfavorable press.

Seemingly out of nowhere, a relatively unknown corporate attorney and former prosecutor rose to oppose Corey in the 2016 Republican Party primary.

Melissa Nelson grew up in Tallahassee, the daughter of a career law enforcement officer who retired as a US marshal. Following her graduation from the University of Florida's Levin College of Law, Nelson went to work for the State Attorney's Office headed by Harry Shorstein. She spent twelve years working an array of cases, prosecuting everything from misdemeanors to grizzly homicides. She resigned ten months after Corey succeeded Shorstein as state attorney in 2009 and took a job with the international law firm McGuireWoods in their Jacksonville office. Nelson credits former prosecutor turned defense attorney Hank Coxe with helping her secure that position.[8]

One of the first cases she was involved with was her firm's representation of Tiger Woods's wife, Elin Nordegren, in her divorce from the golf superstar.

"I was sitting at my desk one Friday night when the managing partner came down and asked me if I could drive him down to Orlando the next morning at 7:00," Nelson recalled. "I was like, 'OK, why are we going?'"

"I can't tell you," was his reply.

It was only when she saw a breaking news alert on her phone that evening about Tiger Woods taking a break from golf that she realized the potential significance of the trip. Barely six months into her new job, she described her role in the Woodses' divorce as essentially "carrying someone's briefcase."[9]

But Nelson soon made her mark at the firm doing Title IX work. She helped defend Florida State University in a lawsuit filed by a woman who said she was raped by FSU quarterback Jameis Winston. The parties eventually settled.

It was her pro bono work with the Cristian Fernandez case that left a lasting impression. When she learned the twelve-year-old was being held in isolation, she called a former colleague at the State Attorney's Office and asked, "What the hell are you guys doing?"[10]

When it became apparent that the Public Defender's Office lacked the resources to handle the case, a group of experienced attorneys, including Coxe and Schulz, stepped in. Despite her strong feelings, Nelson was reluctant to join the group. She did not want to be in an adversarial position with her former colleagues at the State Attorney's Office, many of whom she considered to be her friends.

"The idea of being on the opposite side of the table was not something I was looking to do," Nelson recalled. "When I left [the State Attorney's Office], I was unhappy at how things were going there, but I just wanted to keep my nose down and reinvent myself, and this put me squarely averse to the Office."[11]

But her strong feelings prevailed, and she joined the team as lead contact with the teenager.

She not only became one of his lawyers but his primary visitor and counselor.

The idea of running for public office was never part of Nelson's bucket list or life plan. Nor was running against her former boss, Angela Corey.

"Angela had been a mentor to me," Nelson said. "She was a great trial lawyer. She was a great trainer, she's charismatic and dynamic, but those things, in my mind, didn't translate into good governance. I was really troubled by what I perceived as abuses. I left because of what was going on and never really intended to come back."[12]

Nelson was among a small group who met with other attorneys to see if anyone would be willing to run against Corey. No one stepped up.

With no political experience, little name recognition, and no campaign money to speak of, Nelson made the decision to leave a lucrative job in the private sector to run for public office and challenge Corey in the Republican primary. It was time to stop complaining and to do something about it, she reflected. Once she made the decision, she was all in.

With a campaign that focused on positive messaging and an emphasis on balancing public safety with appropriate sentencing, Nelson's candidacy caught fire. "Tough but fair" became the hallmark of her campaign. She quickly raised more than $1 million with a wide range of support from the legal and business communities, many of whom had grown tired of what they perceived as Corey's polarizing persona. Among her most ardent supporters in the legal community were former state attorney Harry Shorstein and veteran attorneys Hank Coxe and Buddy Schulz, both of whom she collaborated with on the Cristian Fernandez case. She built an unlikely coalition of supporters including some conservative philanthropists alongside more liberal judicial advocates, some of whom winced when she received the endorsement of the National Rifle Association.[13] She proved to be an exceptional campaigner who was often described as elegant, highly intelligent, and charismatic.

Corey, too, had her own base of support, especially among elected officials like Mayor Lenny Curry and Sheriff Mike Williams. She also garnered support from two previous mayors, John Delaney and John Peyton.

"We value her unwavering commitment to taking violent criminals off the streets and holding them accountable," Peyton said in his endorsement.[14] Jacksonville's murder rate had decreased during her administration.

Despite her public feuds and controversies, most political pundits seemed to believe Corey was a virtual lock to win a third term. The race generated an unusually high level of interest, with some Democrats switching party affiliation just to vote in the Republican primary.

In a stunning election result, Nelson defeated Corey by thirty-eight percentage points in what was considered an upset as much for its margin of victory as it was for the fact that the incumbent had been unseated.

"The election caps a dizzying rise for Nelson and an equally shocking fall for Corey," wrote the *Florida Times-Union* in its postelection edition.[15] With no Democratic challenger, Nelson was sworn in as state attorney in January 2017.

The election was destined to change the face of Florida's Fourth Judicial Circuit. As they continued to languish in prison, little did Nathan Myers and Clifford Williams know that that same election was destined to change their fate as well.

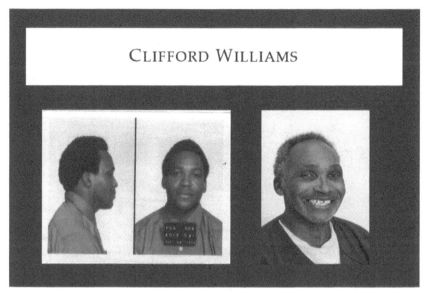

(*Left*) Clifford Williams's prison identification photo, October 1976; (*right*) Williams's prison identification photo years later, before his release. Courtesy of State Attorney's Office, Florida's Fourth Judicial Circuit.

(*Left*) Hubert "Nathan" Myers's prison identification photo, November 1976; (*right*) Myers's prison identification photo years later, before his release. Courtesy of the State Attorney's Office, Florida's Fourth Judicial Circuit.

The block where the shooting took place; the detective is standing in front of the bedroom window of Jeanette Williams and Nina Marshall. A birthday party was taking place at an apartment two buildings down. Courtesy of the State Attorney's Office, Florida's Fourth Judicial Circuit.

Apartment at 1604 Morgan Street where Rachel Jones's birthday party took place during the early-morning hours of March 2, 1976. Courtesy of the State Attorney's Office, Florida's Fourth Judicial Circuit.

Aerial view of the distance between the party location (*left*) and the murder scene (*right*). Courtesy of the State Attorney's Office, Florida's Fourth Judicial Circuit.

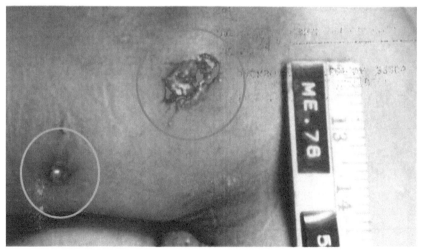

Autopsy photo of the irregular entrance wound on the back of Jeanette Williams's upper right arm, suggesting to the CIR that the bullet may have hit something before impacting the skin. Courtesy of the State Attorney's Office, Florida's Fourth Judicial Circuit.

Crime scene photo of the nightstand next to Nina Marshall's bed that would be viewed as a key piece of evidence in the CIR's reinvestigation. Courtesy of the State Attorney's Office, Florida's Fourth Judicial Circuit.

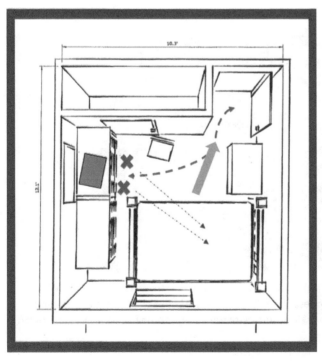

Drawing depicting Nina Marshall's version of how the shooting took place inside the apartment bedroom, with the gunmen firing at the foot of the bed. Courtesy of the State Attorney's Office, Florida's Fourth Judicial Circuit.

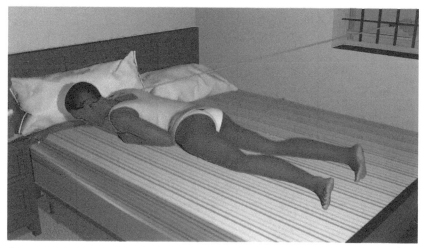

Computer-generated model demonstrating how the path of the fatal bullet to the back of Jeanette Williams's head could have come from outside of the bedroom window. Courtesy of the State Attorney's Office, Florida's Fourth Judicial Circuit.

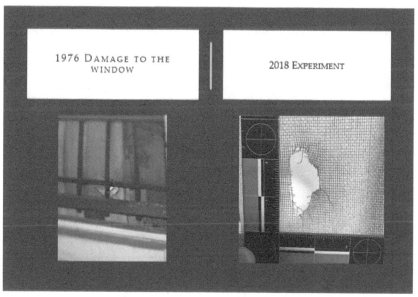

An experiment conducted by Knox & Associates at a gun-firing range was able to replicate similar damage to the window screen from the 1976 murder scene, according to the CIR report. Courtesy of the State Attorney's Office, Florida's Fourth Judicial Circuit.

An emotional Clifford Williams (*right*) is comforted by his nephew Nathan Myers at a press conference moments after the two were exonerated after having spent just shy of forty-three years in prison. Photograph © Will Dickey–USA TODAY NETWORK.

(*Left to right*) Nathan Myers and Clifford Williams are congratulated by CIR director Shelley Thibodeau (*background*) and State Attorney Melissa Nelson (*seated*) at a press conference following their exoneration on March 28, 2019. Courtesy of WJCT News.

12

Conviction Integrity

Attorney Buddy Schulz, formerly of the megafirm Holland & Knight, likes to quote the mantra of the firm's founder, Chesterfield Smith: "Do good, be somebody."[1]

"One of the essential visions of the firm was to be in the community and help those who can't afford access to justice," Schulz said.[2]

As a result, Schulz and his firm had been involved in nearly twenty post-conviction cases, attempting to help defendants prove their innocence, with mixed results. His work brought him into contact with Barry Scheck, co-founder of the Innocence Project.

Scheck, who gained prominence as a member of O. J. Simpson's "Dream Team," started the Innocence Project in 1992 with his co-counsel on the Simpson defense team, Peter Neufeld.

Together they presented arguments of DNA contamination in the case in which Simpson was acquitted. While they never questioned the validity of DNA testing, they did challenge the way the evidence was gathered and processed.

Scheck and Neufeld's role in the highly publicized Simpson case was bound to bring scrutiny to the Innocence Project, whose mission is to "free the staggering number of innocent people who remain incarcerated and to bring reform to the system responsible for their unjust imprisonment."[3]

In an interview with the *Los Angeles Times* commemorating the twentieth anniversary of the trial, Scheck acknowledged that the complexity of the Simpson case "may have muddied the message."[4]

"On the other hand, there were, frankly, uses that can be made of celebrity," Scheck said. "Fame is a good thing to have sometimes if you can put it to good use. The Innocence Project benefited from that."[5]

As of December 22, 2021, the Innocence Project claimed 237 victories, of which 10 percent had been death sentences.[6] Branches of the Innocence Project have been established in numerous states, including Florida.

To assist with their mission, the Innocence Project looked to a new phenomenon happening under the radar. In 2002, California district attorney George Kennedy established the country's first Conviction Integrity Unit (CIU) in Santa Clara, California.[7] Working to correct wrongful convictions was not something new for prosecutors. The first formalized CIU in Santa Clara received little attention despite being responsible for a murder exoneration in 2003 and a robbery exoneration in 2007, the same year the unit was abolished due to a budget cut. (It was reestablished in 2011.)[8]

The most well-known of the early CIUs was created in Dallas, Texas, in 2006 by the county's first Black district attorney, Craig M. Watkins. The Dallas CIU dramatically changed the culture of the Prosecutor's Office. Under Watkins's direction, the Dallas CIU began an internal audit of more than four hundred cases in which a prisoner had requested DNA testing. In less than ten years, thirty-three prisoners were exonerated and freed.[9] The Dallas CIU became the model for other district attorney offices in major cities where prosecutors looked to "right the wrongs of the past."

The Dallas success led to a proliferation of CIUs, aided in part by support from the Innocence Project.

In Florida, Miami-Dade State Attorney Katherine Fernandez Rundle created the Justice Project in 2003 to examine cases that may have resulted in wrongful convictions. While not technically counted among one of the CIUs being established around the country, the South Florida Prosecutor's Office prided itself on being a pioneer in the field of reexamining wrongful convictions.[10]

"We knew the Innocence Project was trying to help implement Conviction Integrity Units across the country, so we asked them to come to Florida to meet with Melissa Nelson," Schulz said.[11]

Sensing an opportunity to establish a CIU in Florida, Schulz wanted the Innocence Project to meet with the newly elected state attorney who had campaigned on a platform to reestablish trust in the Prosecutor's Office.

During the transition before taking office, a meeting was arranged with Nelson in the conference room of the Bedell Firm in downtown Jacksonville, where Hank Coxe practiced law. Among those in attendance were Coxe, Schulz, and attorney Nina Morrison from the Innocence Project.[12]

Nelson was already familiar with the concept of CIUs.

"Even before the campaign I had begun reading about what people were doing in other areas of the country," Nelson recalled.[13]

In her research she learned of a young district attorney, Kenneth Thompson, who started one of the country's most aggressive CIUs in Brooklyn in 2014. The unit discovered a corrupt police detective, Louis Scarcella, who was accused of framing dozens of innocent men for crimes they did not commit. By 2018, fourteen individuals had their convictions overturned involving Scarcella with many more under review.[14]

"It begs the question as a prosecutor, what's our responsibility looking backward?" Nelson said.[15]

Members of the Florida Bar are governed by the rules of professional conduct, which provides that prosecutors have an ongoing obligation to act upon "new credible and material evidence that creates a reasonable likelihood that a convicted defendant did not commit the offense for which he was convicted. Therefore, prosecutors have a unique obligation both ethically and as officers of the court to act on evidence of innocence whenever it avails itself to ensure that no factually innocent person remains wrongfully convicted."[16]

Nelson had her own experience.

"When I was here as a prosecutor, I handled a postconviction investigation of a homicide, and the Innocence Project was on the other side. We started working in partnership doing testing, and we ultimately abandoned the charges and dropped the case because of the way the DNA testing panned out. That's when I got to know Nina Morrison."[17]

At the meeting at the Bedell Firm, Nelson said they were just "spitballing" the idea of establishing a CIU in the Fourth Circuit, "not because I felt there was a bastion of wrongful convictions, because I didn't. I just thought this might go a long way toward building trust. That was my biggest priority in coming back, restoring the reputation of the office."[18]

Ultimately, Nelson said she knew there was no money to create such a unit. And, she knew there would be legitimate skepticism within the office she was preparing to lead.

"Here I am brand-new, and if I go in and say, 'Hey, I'm going to take money that otherwise I could spend on your merit raises and I'm going to give it to somebody else who's going to be looking over your shoulder' . . . I had just enough walking-around sense to know that would be a recipe for disaster."[19]

So, the idea of a CIU was filed away, at least for the time being.

In November 2016, three months after the election but before assuming office, Nelson met with the editorial board of the *Florida Times-Union* newspaper. The meeting included some of the news staff. She remembered following some sage advice she was given while on the campaign trail—stay on message and be disciplined.

It worked for most of the meeting.

"We were done, and I was relieved I hadn't said anything off point," Nelson recalled.[20]

As she was about to walk out the door, reporter Ben Conarck offered up one final question.

"Have you ever thought about a Conviction Integrity Unit?"

Nelson was excited to answer the question.

"Yes, as a matter of fact I have," was her reply. "That is something I am very, very interested in. We've already had a meeting about it, and we've talked to the Innocence Project."[21]

Within moments a headline scrolled across the *Times-Union*'s website: "Under Melissa Nelson, Jacksonville Prosecutors Could Search for Wrongful Convictions."[22]

The article went on to say how Nelson was considering setting up a CIU at the local State Attorney's Office, which would be the first such unit in Florida.

"I mean, like, we are leaving the paper and getting into the car and there's this headline," Nelson recalled. "I thought, my God, well this is an idea I haven't talked to anybody in the office broadly about. I don't have the money to do this, and now I am publicly accountable to something."[23]

The news traveled fast. The next day Nelson received a phone call from John Hollway of the Quattrone Center for the Fair Administration of Justice at the University of Pennsylvania Carey Law School.

"He had been monitoring news about Conviction Integrity Units and said he'd love to help," Nelson said.[24] Hollway had set up a guide for best practices for these units and offered his services to the incoming state attorney.

"I told him I didn't have any money to consult with him, and he said he'd do it for free," Nelson recalled.[25]

As it turns out, Hollway wasn't the only one monitoring the news. In the library of the Sumter Correctional Institution Nathan Myers's "jailhouse lawyer," Tony Brown, was reading his batch of daily newspapers including the *Florida Times-Union*. He saw the article and immediately went to his friend Nathan.

He told Myers, "You might want to read this."[26]

He showed him the article about Nelson intending to create a CIU. "You need to write to her right now," Brown said.[27]

After decades of frustration, Myers sensed a glimmer of hope.

In January 2017, he penned the following introduction:

> Dear State Attorney,
>
> I pray you please excuse my intrusion. I am writing this letter after reading an article in the Florida Times-Union in which you were starting a group to seek out and reverse wrongful convictions by establishing a Conviction Integrity Unit. I can only pray for the assistance of the Conviction Integrity Unit to prove I am innocent of having committed the crimes I was wrongly convicted of. For the past forty-two years I've been in prison faced with the prospect of dying in a prison cell for a crime I had nothing to do with. I was 18 years of age at the time of these crimes. Today, I am 59 years old having spent 42 years in prison for a crime I did not and could not have committed.[28]

As he sent the letter off detailing the history of his case, Myers had to wonder . . . with so many disappointments and dead ends, would anybody even listen?

13

A Fox in the Henhouse

Now that the cat had been let out of the bag about establishing Florida's first Conviction Integrity Unit, newly elected state attorney Melissa Nelson set out on a mission.

Her comments to the *Florida Times-Union* editorial board had made headlines.

"I felt a sense of urgency, like I've got to make this happen. I had this public accountability," she said.[1]

Her first priority was funding. She delivered a concept paper to state Senator Rob Bradley Jr. of the North Central Florida legislative delegation.

"It was my first-ever foray into lobbying," she recalled. "I apparently offended a lot of elected officials in the State of Florida because usually we move together as a group when we ask for money. I was going rogue without even appreciating that I was screwing up etiquette."[2]

Despite her lack of experience, Nelson's stunning margin of victory earned her some cachet and support in Tallahassee, where they sensed the headwinds of a new political force in the Fourth Judicial Circuit.

As a result, the Florida Legislature awarded her office a long-term, recurring, $380,000 funding commitment for the state's first Conviction Integrity Unit. There was an initial bump in the road when some other funding for her office was stripped, but the long-term deal took some of the pressure off in more ways than one.

"When we announced it to the office, we were able to say, 'This money is earmarked and I'm not allowed to spend it anywhere else, so I'm not taking it out of your pocket,'" Nelson said.[3] While true, the explanation wouldn't ease all the tensions within the State Attorney's Office, as time would tell.

With funding in place and the concept hammered out, Nelson set her sights on finding the right person to run the unit. She was aware of the challenges within the office.

"I knew it was going to take a special personality, so it mattered who we brought over," Nelson recalled. "It couldn't be somebody who collectively the office didn't trust."[4]

Although she initially envisioned someone with both defense and prosecutorial experience, Nelson ended up targeting a veteran defense attorney with no experience as a prosecutor.

Shelley Thibodeau had seen a *Florida Times-Union* article that the newly elected state attorney planned to establish Florida's first Conviction Integrity Unit. The diminutive twenty-year veteran defense attorney was more than a little skeptical.

"I remember sort of thinking, that's absurd," Thibodeau recalled. "Especially since one of the articles referred to their looking for a 'wrongful conviction czar.' I had some trepidation about whether something like that was going to work in Jacksonville."[5]

Thibodeau had grown up in Orlando, Florida, living the magical childhood of a Disney World kid. Her father was a Vietnam veteran who was hired by Disney in their accounts-receivable department shortly after he returned from the war.[6]

"Disney, back in the '70s and '80s, took really good care of their employees, so my brother and I had our birthday parties there, and we could bring as many kids as we wanted," Thibodeau recalled. "And on Friday and Saturday they would have family nights where families could bring their children to the Contemporary Hotel to see the Disney movies like *The Parent Trap* and others."[7]

Thibodeau studied law at Florida State University, where she participated in a child advocacy clinic. Her experiences there left a lasting impression.

"I saw a thirteen-year-old kid who had been arrested for stealing another student's brownie at school and putting it in his backpack," she recalled. "And I was thinking, my God, we're labeling thirteen-year-olds as criminals for stealing a brownie. I mean, it just blew my mind."[8]

Another case involved a fifteen-year-old who was arrested for skateboarding on school grounds.

The teenager told Thibodeau he didn't think he was on school grounds. Thibodeau, still a law student, went to City Hall, pulled the real estate plat, and determined the teenager was in fact not on school property. Her research helped win the case.[9]

"It made such an impact on me because the kid's mother, who was a single mom, told me there was no way she would ever be able to afford private counsel, so she was just going through the system," Thibodeau said. "You put your faith in the system and hope for the best.

"I came from a very middle-class family and to see these kids being arrested for what I perceived to be such ridiculous things . . . I decided to find employment doing criminal defense work."[10]

Her husband, Dave, whom she met at law school, landed a job in Jacksonville, where the couple settled. After more than twenty years as a defense attorney, Thibodeau was surprised when she was approached about heading up the state's first Conviction Integrity Unit.

"Well, you know, Melissa['s enthusiasm] is very infectious and contagious, and she explained to me her vision of why she thought this was important," Thibodeau recalled. "She is pretty convincing, and I thought to myself, she's asking a defense attorney to be the head of this unit inside the State Attorney's Office, so you know how serious she was about what she wanted to accomplish."[11]

Thibodeau's years as defense counsel helped forge her own perspective.

"You know it [wrongful conviction] sometimes happens, and you pray that you are a talented enough defense attorney to spot it and correct the injustice before they are convicted."[12]

She recognized the advantages of working inside the State Attorney's Office.

"When you are a defense attorney, you are sort of on the outside chipping away at it," she reasoned. "I saw this new opportunity as a chance to chip away at it from the inside and know you have a chance to be part of something very powerful. I mean, it's really been my calling to help people who are for the most part voiceless."[13]

Despite her initial trepidation, Thibodeau agreed to head the newly created unit. Her appointment was met with public praise.

"She's a hard worker," attorney Rhonda Peoples-Waters told the *Florida Times-Union*. "She's known to do the research. I definitely have so much respect for her. I thought it spoke volumes that Melissa hired her."[14]

Betsy White, a constitutional lawyer practicing in Jacksonville, echoed those sentiments to the *Florida Times-Union*. "She brings the experience the position needs. . . . We need someone who will not be afraid to go places where other people would hesitate to go."[15]

While the public praise was palpable, there were already silent rumblings within the State Attorney's Office. More than one questioned, "What are we doing here?"

The response was not unexpected. John Hollway, the University of Pennsylvania professor whom Nelson had relied on to provide a list of best practices, had cautioned as much.

"It takes time to convince the attorneys in your office that the unit is there to help you do your job better and not to second-guess your decisions," he said.[16]

Meanwhile, there was work to be done. Publicity about the newly formed Conviction Integrity Unit had generated a surge of responses. As Thibodeau sat at her desk to begin her new role in January 2018, there were already eighty letters waiting for her review. Somewhere in the stack was the well-composed, prayerful plea from Nathan Myers about the Morgan Street murder more than four decades earlier.

14

Irony

From the moment she arrived at the State Attorney's Office to begin her new role as director of Florida's first Conviction Integrity Unit, Shelley Thibodeau could sense the uneasiness within the office.

"I could feel it," she recalled. "I tried to express to people within the office that I'm not an internal affairs officer. I'd like to think most prosecutors aren't trying to convict innocent people. Sometimes, for whatever reason, the system fails. It's not personal, but if we can correct the system . . . we need to correct it."[1]

Her boss, Melissa Nelson, likened it to an airplane crash investigation, according to Thibodeau: "We are not blaming the pilot. We aren't blaming that person that put the piece of equipment on the airplane. We are talking about airplane crashes in terms of a systems failure."[2]

Nevertheless, the internal resistance, albeit subtle, was hard to ignore. It was all the more reason to be highly selective in determining the cases to review.

As she sat down at her desk on day one, the stack of letters that awaited her seemed unwieldy. It had been months since the first newspaper article appeared about the creation of a Conviction Integrity Unit in Florida's Fourth Judicial Circuit. (The local office adopted the name Conviction Integrity Review [CIR].)

As she began the daunting task of sifting through the pile, Thibodeau was looking for some sense of perspective. "What exactly am I dealing with here?" she wondered.[3]

Most of the petitions were a couple of paragraphs asking for someone in the newly created division to please review their file. As she worked her way down the stack, she came across a petition that was different in tone and substance. It was specific and meticulous.

"What distinguished Nathan Myers's petition from the rest of what I was reading was the amount of detail," Thibodeau recalled. "It just struck me as being plausible. Why I wasn't getting that same amount of detail in the other letters didn't make a whole lot of sense to me."[4]

In his petition, Myers, with the help of Tony Brown, set forth his argument, complete with an array of supporting documents including a hand-drawn diagram of the apartment where the shooting occurred.

"I'm thinking to myself that if I'm in prison and I've been wrongfully convicted, this is the sort of thing I would be doing to try and convince someone of my innocence," Thibodeau said.[5]

In the petition, Myers detailed how none of the witnesses who could have placed him and his uncle at a nearby party at the time of the shooting were ever called to testify. He described how none of the physical evidence, which pointed to the shooting coming from outside the apartment, was ever presented at the trial.

In short, Myers used the opportunity to send Thibodeau all the case information he had compiled in four decades in prison to support his innocence in the hope that he had finally found an attentive ear.

After reviewing Myers's petition, Thibodeau began looking at the trial transcript.

Piece by piece, Myers's version of the story seemed to be borne out by what Thibodeau was reading in the transcript.

"There was no physical evidence that linked either one of them to these crimes," Thibodeau said. "The only evidence that the State Attorney's Office put forth at trial was the word of the surviving victim."[6]

Thibodeau said she soon became "obsessed with doing a deep dive into what happened."[7]

The trial transcript revealed another awkward detail, which those familiar with the case already knew; the prosecutor representing the State in the 1976 trial was Hank Coxe, the same Hank Coxe who was instrumental in helping elect Melissa Nelson as state attorney and who was a catalyst for the creation of the very CIR unit that was now revisiting his case.

After a highly successful stint as an assistant state attorney, Coxe left the Prosecutor's Office in 1981 and turned his attention to defense work. Over time he became one of the most recognizable and influential faces in the Jacksonville legal community, taking on high-profile cases and assuming numerous leadership roles including president of both the Jacksonville Bar Association and the Florida Bar Association.

The recipient of numerous judicial awards, Coxe also served on the Florida Judicial Qualifications Commission and the Florida Supreme Court Innocence Commission. He was known as much for his pro bono work as he was for some of his more famous clients like former Jacksonville Jaguar wide receiver Jimmy Smith.

Nelson and Thibodeau did not approach Coxe right away. They wanted to ensure they had their ducks in a row and that the Myers-Williams case was indeed worth pursuing as the first case to be handled by the newly created CIR unit.

Once they were convinced, it fell to Nelson to break the news to her longtime supporter.

"She called me up one day and said I need to come talk to you," Coxe recalled.[8]

Nelson headed over to the Bedell Firm building on Adams Street, where Coxe practiced as a director of the firm. The stately, four-column building has a rich history. It was the former home of the Carnegie Library, the building that served as Jacksonville's main library branch from 1905 until 1965.[9] Over the years it was no doubt the site of many meetings of legal and political power brokers.

Nelson took a seat in the same conference room where less than two years earlier she had met with Coxe and others to discuss the possibility of a Conviction Integrity Unit (CIU) in the Fourth Judicial Circuit.

"She asked me if I remembered somebody named Boonie," Coxe said.[10]

Coxe immediately recited to Nelson details of the case he had tried more than four decades ago:

"Clifford 'Boonie' Williams was codefendant with Nathan Myers . . . tried in the mid-70s before Judge Cliff Shepard and they had guns blazing inside the apartment and she went to the hospital, and she scribbled a note to the patrolman that said 'Boonie' or something like that."[11]

Nelson asked Coxe how he remembered the details so many years later.

Coxe responded, "I'm a big believer that if you're gonna ask somebody to be sentenced to death as a prosecutor, you better remember the details. That may sound presumptuous and arrogant, but it's true."[12]

Coxe then asked Nelson, "What's going on?"

Nelson told Coxe about the letter and petition they had received from Nathan Myers and that Shelley Thibodeau had been working on it and "we think they are probably innocent."

"Do you really?" Coxe asked. "Well, you can't ask me if I agree and if I've been sitting around for forty-plus years knowing I put two innocent people in prison."[13]

He did not, however, throw a roadblock. Quite the contrary.

"I am not about to say you're wrong or you shouldn't do it," Coxe told Nelson. "That would be totally contrary to everything we've talked about since you got elected. If there's anything I can provide or help with, have at it."[14]

Coxe added an additional, personal statement. "If they didn't do it, I'll deal with it."[15]

Almost immediately he began rethinking the case.

"You are not human to have had that conversation and just go back to your regular work without rethinking it . . . a lot," Coxe said.[16]

There was nothing in his revisiting the case that caused him to change his mind about the outcome.

"I wouldn't have ever prosecuted them if I thought they were innocent," he said.[17]

He decided against reaching out to any of the detectives or other law enforcement officials who were involved in the original investigation.

"That was their job," he said, referring to the CIU. "That'll take its course."[18]

Coxe did go home and tell his wife, Mary, who also worked in the State Attorney's Office in the mid-1970s and had sat in on the Myers-Williams trial.

"You won't believe the conversation I had at work today," he told her.

Coxe said his wife reacted just as anybody would have who was involved with the case at the time.

"Oh, bullshit! There's no way those guys didn't do it."[19]

15

Reconstruction

The more she dug, the more convinced Shelley Thibodeau became that Nathan Myers and Clifford Williams had been wrongfully convicted. Nothing she read about the physical evidence supported Nina Marshall's eyewitness account that Williams and Myers had stood at the foot of the bed and fired their guns at the two sleeping women. To the contrary, the physical evidence strongly suggested the bullets came from outside the apartment through the bedroom window, which had been shattered, with broken glass found under the window and on top of the victims' bed.

The aluminum screen outside the bedroom window had a hole in it with the prongs pointing inward, further suggesting that a bullet traveled from outside to inside. A hole in the bottom corner of the window frame had traces of gun residue.

Then there was the crime lab analysis that indicated all six bullets recovered were fired from a single .38 caliber gun. Marshall had been adamant in her testimony that there were two gunmen in the bedroom and that both had fired shots. Yet neither Williams nor Myers had any trace of gunpowder residue when they were tested a few hours after the shooting.

Perhaps most compelling were the alibi witnesses, more than thirty of them, mostly Black women, none of whom were called to testify despite having told investigators that Williams and Myers were at Rachel Jones's birthday party when the shots were heard. And while the community in and around Morgan Street was known for its drug activity, what would have been the motive for protecting Williams and Myers if the men had killed one of their own, Jeanette "Baldie" Williams? Most of the witnesses interviewed seemed to have been fond of "Baldie" and would have no reason to protect her killer.

For Thibodeau, believing the men had been wrongfully convicted was one thing. Building a case for their exoneration four decades later was quite another. Many of the key players were no longer alive, including the only known eyewitness, Nina Marshall. Gone, too, were many of the alibi witnesses, the defense attorneys, and Nathaniel Lawson, who allegedly admitted to several others that he was the one responsible for the shooting.

"I'm thinking to myself that these men went to prison when I was only six years old, and they've spent almost my entire lifetime in prison for something they didn't do," recalled Thibodeau. "So, it became very urgent for me to continue my investigation as quickly as possible so that we could get to a place where the courts decide what they are going to do."[1]

One of her first steps was to try and track down any physical evidence that might still be around forty years later.

"We went over to the property room multiple times and thought there must be something we can look over for ourselves," Thibodeau recalled. "You know you hear about these cases around the country where there's been a box in some closet somewhere. Maybe we could find something to DNA-test."[2]

Much to her disappointment, there was no such box in this case.

With the help of investigator Ernest Edwards, Thibodeau then spent the next several months knocking on doors trying to locate and speak with some of the alibi witnesses who might still be alive. Most were deceased. Over time, Thibodeau and Edwards developed a network of contacts that helped them locate some of the witnesses.

"Some just didn't want to be involved because they had moved past the lifestyle they had been living in the 1970s and had moved on with their lives," Thibodeau said.[3]

Of the original alibi witnesses listed on discovery by the defense, Thibodeau was able to locate ten: Dorothy Benson, Kay Frances Brown, Belinda Bryant, Pauline Dawson, Joann Fleming, Ella Ruth Mattox, Rico Rivers, Vanessa Snype, Deborah White, and Vincent Williams.[4]

Their memories were not great in most cases.

"The best I could get from the majority of them is that they remembered Clifford and Nathan being at the party," Thibodeau said of the responses. "But if you want to know details like what they were wearing or whatever, I couldn't tell you."[5]

While the details may have been scant, no one recanted their original statements to investigators that the two men were at the party when the shots were heard.

"I never heard anybody tell me they were pressured or bribed to come forward," Thibodeau said.[6]

What did strike Thibodeau was that more than forty years later, the women interviewed still expressed a fondness for the victim, Jeanette "Baldie" Williams. Many had attended her funeral and signed the guest book. Some told Thibodeau, "This was my friend, and if Clifford and Nathan were involved, I certainly would have said so."[7]

The same fondness did not extend to Nina Marshall, who was well known as a drug dealer and prostitute and had a reputation for ripping off other drug dealers. None of the witnesses interviewed had anything negative to say about Nathan Myers. On the other hand, no one had particularly good things to say about Clifford Williams, who was also well known for his reputation as a drug dealer.[8]

One of those interviewed by the CIR was Joann Fleming, who lived on Morgan Street in the apartment next door to Rachel Jones and who was there the night of the shooting. After more than forty years she had a specific and clear memory of seeing Clifford Williams at the party when the shots were heard. She was firm in her belief that he was not the shooter.[9]

Also interviewed by the CIR was Vincent Williams, a cousin to both Myers and Williams. He had specific memories of the party and the early-morning shooting. He remembers Clifford Williams being in the kitchen and Nathan Myers in the living room. They were the only two people he knew at the party, and since they were family members, he had "reason to make a mental note of the events," according to the CIR investigation.[10]

He left the party early because his parents had not wanted him to attend in the first place. When he subsequently learned his cousins had been arrested for the murder, he went to Clifford Williams's attorney's office to tell them what he knew. He doesn't remember ever speaking to detectives or prosecutors and was never called to testify. As with so many in this case, Vincent Williams has his own criminal history. He is a convicted felon for possession of cocaine and worthless checks, according to the CIR.[11]

While it was only a piece of the reinvestigation, Thibodeau's interviews with the alibi witnesses felt compelling.

"There were forty or so people, who in their heart of hearts believed that Nathan and Clifford were not involved in this because they knew they were at the birthday party . . . and for whatever reason their stories were discounted, and it happens to be the majority of them were African American women," Thibodeau said. "I think that happens a lot in the Black community . . . they know what's going on and yet they feel disenfranchised because nobody is listening to what they are saying."[12]

Four decades later, Thibodeau hoped to give them a voice that could potentially help free Nathan Myers and Clifford Williams.

16

To Tell the Truth

Nathan Myers remembers the stern admonition he heard from Shelley Thibodeau.

"If I ever find out that you've lied to me, I'm done," he recalls her saying.[1]

Thibodeau has her own recollection.

"I don't know if I said it quite like that, but probably at some point I told him if I find out you've been untruthful, then I'm not going down this road for somebody who's not being straightforward," she said. "I don't know that I ever caught him telling me something that I couldn't substantiate or that I wasn't able to corroborate."[2]

That trust would eventually be put to a test with a polygraph. Thibodeau had waited until her unit's investigation of the case was well under way before contacting Myers to discuss his willingness to take a polygraph. It would be her first-ever face-to-face meeting with the incarcerated defendant.

Despite her own strong feelings, she didn't want to get Myers's hopes up. Myers and Williams had spent more than four decades in prison with little chance of having their case ever revisited. She was trying to temper her own expectations. Myers would sometimes write to Thibodeau just to make sure the investigation was moving along. Her initial responses were cautious and circumspect.

"When I finally reached out to Nathan, I had a phone call with him, along with my investigator Ernest Edwards, and I asked if he would be willing to come to Jacksonville for a polygraph examination to be conducted by the Jacksonville Sheriff's Office," Thibodeau recalled.[3]

Myers agreed, and a court order was obtained to bring both Nathan and his uncle Clifford to Jacksonville.

Virtually all the correspondence to this point had been between Myers and Thibodeau.

"I was wondering to myself, why is Clifford not contacting me more. Why is it all Nathan-driven?" Thibodeau said.[4]

It was clear Myers had taken the lead role in pursuing the exoneration efforts. Williams's declining health and cognitive issues may have played a role. While he, too, agreed to a polygraph, it was determined during the pretest phase that Williams was unable to cognitively perform the test, so it was terminated by the examiner out of concern the results would not be valid.[5]

As Nathan Myers was brought into the State Attorney's Office the day before the polygraph, Thibodeau was able to form her own first impressions.

"Right away you are just drawn to him," Thibodeau said of Nathan. "He's likable and seemed very straightforward."[6]

Thibodeau and Investigator Edwards brought Myers up-to-date on their investigation, including their interviews with some of the surviving alibi witnesses. Thibodeau recalled that Myers kept expressing his gratitude over and over that after so many years someone was willing to look at his case.[7]

For his part, Myers was confident but nevertheless nervous. There had been so many dead ends in his quest for freedom, so much disappointment. He knew the polygraph results would weigh heavily, especially in his relationship with Thibodeau and the CIR team.

"At first, I was a little nervous," Myers admitted. "Then I asked, 'What am I nervous for? I just need to answer the questions correctly.' I didn't have anything to hide."[8]

It was unusual for a defendant to undergo a polygraph conducted by the Jacksonville Sheriff's Office. "What crazy defense attorney is going to allow their client to run on a JSO polygraph?" Thibodeau mused.[9]

Pursuant to protocol, Myers was interviewed and then asked a series of three questions:[10]

Question: "Did you shoot either of those women?"

Myers: "No."

Question: "Did you shoot either of those women in May of 1976?"

Myers: "No."

Question: "Did you shoot either of those women at 1550 Morgan Street, Apt. 1?"

Myers: "No."[11]

Myers waited anxiously for the result. After a few tense minutes, Investigator Edwards returned with a thumbs-up.[12]

The examiner reported that Myers showed no deception in his answers.

"After analyzing the recorded data, this examiner reached the conclusion that the subject's responses to the relevant questions during the examination were consistent with that of 'No Deception Indicated,'" concluded the report submitted by Detective E. K. Moore of the Jacksonville Sheriff's Office.[13]

"I don't want to speak out of turn, but she [the examiner] must have had some feelings about it because later she would ask me for updates about the investigation . . . 'how was it going and where are you in the process?'" Thibodeau recalled. "You know, she must have felt strongly about it that she would reach out."[14]

The polygraph results may have reenforced Thibodeau's belief that Myers and his uncle had been wrongfully convicted. But in full context, it was far from conclusive and certainly not enough on its own to warrant an exoneration. As a rule, polygraph results are generally inadmissible in court unless all parties have stipulated otherwise. But it was another investigative tool, the results of which seemed to fall in line with other evidence supporting Myers and Williams's claim they were innocent of the 1976 shooting.

Although still in uncharted waters, Thibodeau knew she would need much more.

"What's the threshold for innocence?" she would ask herself. "For guilt, it's beyond a reasonable doubt. For innocence . . . we are still grappling with that."[15]

With no DNA to exculpate, it would take more than a polygraph and interviews with alibi witnesses to build a case for exoneration. It would take some old-fashioned experiments and some cutting-edge technology conducted in a basement laboratory to help move the case along.

17

Shots Heard 'Round the Block

At first, the idea seemed a little crazy.

In mid-2018, investigators with the Conviction Integrity Review (CIR) unit paid a visit to the same apartment at 1550 Morgan Street where Jeanette "Baldie" Williams had been murdered and Nina Marshall wounded back on May 2, 1976.

Not much had changed in the neighborhood.

"These buildings were the same configuration and the same material as they were back in 1976," Thibodeau recalled.[1] The front bedroom window at the 1550 Morgan Street apartment was still cracked as it appeared in the 1976 crime scene photographs.

The area in and around Morgan Street is still a high-crime zone with plenty of drug and gang activity nearby. (Once, after his release from prison, Nathan Myers drove back to the old neighborhood but was afraid to get out of his car.)[2]

The CIR investigators made three separate visits to the apartment to take pictures and measurements. The tenant was very accommodating, according to Thibodeau.[3]

Next, came an unusual request.

"We know this sounds a little crazy, but we'd like to fire a .38 caliber revolver inside your bedroom," Thibodeau told the tenant. Thibodeau explained the reasons behind the request and permission was granted.[4]

"She told us if someone is in prison for something they shouldn't be there for, then of course I'm going to allow you to come in," is how Thibodeau remembered the conversation.[5]

The test-fire experiment came about as result of a meeting Thibodeau had with two independent consultants in the field of forensic reconstruction. Michael Knox was a former police officer and detective with the Jacksonville Sheriff's Office who had established his own firm, Knox & Associates, which specialized in ballistics and shooting incident reconstruction. Among those working with Knox was Tom Brady, a former, seasoned Naval Criminal Investigative Service (NCIS) forensic investigator with extensive experience in overseeing crime scene teams. Together, they proposed a series of experiments aimed at helping determine what really happened at the crime scene on May 2, 1976.

"Not all attorneys appreciate forensics and what forensics can bring to the table, objectively," Brady said. "If the forensics don't fit your narrative, just accept it. But Shelley was very open to the use of forensics in a holistic sense."[6]

Even if it didn't fit the narrative that Williams and Myers were innocent, Thibodeau was ready to proceed.

On November 14, 2018, the CIR team, accompanied by Knox and Brady, arrived at 1550 Morgan Street to conduct their sound experiment. Some of the investigators remained inside the apartment. Others, including Thibodeau, moved about fifty yards away to the nearby apartment at 1604 Morgan Street where Rachel Jones held her birthday party the night of the shooting. A digital audio-recording device was positioned at the site of the party's location.[7]

Without any warning as to timing, two shots were fired from inside the bedroom of the 1550 Morgan Street apartment. The sound was clearly audible to those standing immediately outside the apartment building.[8]

However, those stationed at Rachel Jones's old apartment could only detect the faintest of sounds, "not measurably louder than the ambient noise level," according to the Knox report.[9]

"You could hardly hear anything," Thibodeau said, adding that the experiment was conducted before noon on a quiet day.[10]

Again, without warning, two shots from the same .38 caliber revolver were fired from outside the apartment window at 1550 Morgan Street.

As those shots were fired, "It was clear as day that something had gone on," Thibodeau said from her vantage point at the front door of Rachel Jones's apartment.[11]

The two shots fired from outside the bedroom window were "clearly perceptible on the audio recording . . . and six shots fired in succession, likely would have been loud and distinct enough to get the attention of the people at the party," the CIR concluded.[12]

To the CIR, the results of the sound experiment further corroborated the statements of the alibi witnesses who claimed they heard loud gunfire, supporting the position that shots were fired from outside the bedroom window as opposed to inside the apartment as Nina Marshall had alleged.

One piece of evidence that seemed to contradict the notion that the shots came from outside was the metal screen on the exterior of the bedroom window. Detectives originally assigned to the case maintained that the hole in the screen could not have been caused by six bullets being fired from outside the window.

"I'm no gun expert," Thibodeau admitted. "I'm thinking that if you can't get six bullets through a screen and have the kind of damage present, then maybe we are on the wrong track."[13]

To test their theory, a metal screen was purchased from a salvage yard and taken to a firing range. Shooting at contact range, Knox was able to replicate the same damage to the screen as seen in 1976.[14]

"We tried to see if we could get six bullets at close range through a hole like that," Thibodeau said. "The further you backed up, you couldn't get six bullets through a single hole, but if you were very close, you could get it, which is what I would envision someone's doing. They're not shooting from fifteen feet away."[15]

Through this experiment the CIR believed it had determined it was possible that all six shots could be fired from outside the window and form only a single tear in the screen.[16]

"We were doing everything we could to try and validate the thought process because I knew people would be questioning what we were doing," Thibodeau recalled. "I wanted to make sure I was dotting all the *i*'s and crossing all the *t*'s, and that's when we got Jim McMillan involved down in the basement."[17]

The basement of the State Attorney's Office, an eighty-eight-year-old former US Post Office building, is the home of the Trial Support Services division for the Fourth Judicial Circuit. In reality, it resembles a crime lab/museum with delicate re-creations of crime scenes and detailed evidence presentations that bring to life an otherwise dark, cavernous setting. There are no windows, but there is plenty to explore.

The division is a one-man operation run by Jim McMillan, a veteran law enforcement officer turned forensic artist whose visual exhibits and re-creations have been used by prosecutors to present to juries in some of Jacksonville's highest-profile cases. Here you can find shadow boxes with shell casings and miniature models of complex crime scenes.

"My biggest motivation is to try to present the evidence to the jury in the way that they can best understand what they were being shown and told so they can arrive at the right decision, whatever that might be," said McMillan. "I tell people I work for the State Attorney's Office; they pay me, but I really feel like I work for the jury when I'm doing all of these things."[18]

McMillan worked for the Jacksonville Sheriff's Office for twenty-seven years, the last sixteen of which he was a composite artist. The self-taught McMillan is the son of former Jacksonville sheriff Jim McMillan, who headed the JSO from 1986 to 1996.

After his retirement from the Sheriff's Office, the younger McMillan did contract work for the State Attorney's Office before Melissa Nelson convinced him to join the office full-time. He was accustomed to having his work used by prosecutors to present to juries so they might better understand evidence being presented in a case.[19]

When Thibodeau asked McMillan to review the files of the Myers-Williams case, she did so without offering any preconceived notions or hint of where she was headed.

"At this point, I'm convinced, but Melissa asked me to consult with Jim, so I did," Thibodeau said. "I didn't want him to be polluted, so to speak, so I just gave him some documents to look at and asked him to form his thoughts and conclusions."[20]

"She didn't tell me a lot," McMillan recalled, "other than that she had been looking at this case and she wanted another perspective and another set of eyes. Almost immediately, I was struck by things that bothered me."[21]

From his initial review, McMillan said Nina Marshall's account that the shooting happened inside the apartment at the foot of the bed didn't add up. He began working with computer models to re-create the crime scene and the trajectory of the bullets.[22]

Wanting to get a more realistic sense of the space inside the apartment, McMillan laid masking tape on the floor of his basement office. Using crime scene photos and actual measurements taken from the apartment, McMillan re-created the entire bedroom including all the furniture, walls, and the window. A first impression was that the bedroom was very small, approximately nine feet by twelve feet. Given the room's contents, there would have been little space for two grown men to move around once inside. The bedroom door was located directly across from the head of the bed.

"One of the things that struck me is that if your intention is to kill two people who are asleep in the bed, why would you walk to the farthest part of the room when you could have just entered the bedroom door and put the gun right up to the bed, pow pow, and leave," McMillan said. "But that's not what she claimed happened. It just made no sense."[23]

Marshall had testified that the two gunmen fired shots from in front of the television set near the bottom of the bed.

"When you saw the room configuration in Jim's office, it was even more clear how ludicrous it was," Thibodeau said, referring to Marshall's account of the shooting. "If you really wanted to kill someone, you could have walked right in the bedroom door, put the gun right up to bodies, fired the shots, and left. You wouldn't have done all these histrionics of going down to the bottom of the bed."[24]

But there was more, according to McMillan. No matter how hard he tried, he couldn't reconcile the trajectory of the bullets and the wound paths as having come from shots fired at the end of the bed, as Marshall had alleged.

Using an animated 3D computer program called Poser, McMillan was able to create various scenarios of body movements and bullet trajectory. McMillan purchased the program at his own expense, hoping to shed some additional light on what happened the night of the shooting.[25]

Believing the shots could have been fired from outside the bedroom window, McMillan set up a 3D model, tracking where the bodies were when the shots were fired and where they ended up.

"I could hit every bullet hole from that one hole in the screen," McMillan said. "There might have been a hundred other movements that might have missed, but it was possible that it came from there. I couldn't do that from the TV. It just wasn't there."[26]

McMillan took it a step further. Using an artist's drop cloth and a pillow, he lay on the floor of his basement office with a four-foot dowel and tried to figure out a position that would line up the shots and the wound paths as having come from the direction of the TV. He was unable to do so.[27]

"The foundation of this whole case was one witness," McMillan said. "I read her depositions and her court testimony, and I'm not going to go so far as to say she lied, but she was wrong," McMillan said. Referencing the various discrepancies in Marshall's statements about how the shooting occurred, McMillan said, "She doesn't even know how many times she got shot. The only thing she got right is that she was shot."[28]

McMillan said his review of the case kept him awake at night.

"Once we were convinced that this was a wrongful conviction, it was like we needed to get them out yesterday," he said.[29]

The CIR took its computer modeling and the original medical examiner's photographs from 1976 to the city's chief medical examiner, Dr. Valerie Rao.

The medical examiner at the time of the shooting, Dr. Peter Lipkovic, told detectives in 1976 that based on his examination of the victim, the shots would not have come from the window but rather were "highly consistent" with the statements of Nina Marshall as to where the shots had been fired.[30]

"We just wanted to see if there was something we missed," Thibodeau said.[31]

When reviewing the original photographs, Dr. Rao pointed out that the entrance wound on the back of Jeanette Williams's upper arm was irregular and not circular, suggesting the bullet hit something else before impacting the skin.[32]

To Thibodeau, this simply affirmed her conclusion that the bullet hit the glass, the screen, or the window frame before striking Jeanette Williams.

McMillan's 3D computer modeling seemed to demonstrate the path of the fatal bullet that struck the back of Jeanette Williams's head tracked back to the bedroom window.[33]

"I've been a part of putting some really bad people in prison," McMillan said reflecting on his years of service to law enforcement. "But this is the best thing I've ever done."[34]

Knox & Associates, the forensic reconstruction firm that participated in the sound experiments and the computer modeling, issued a report to the CIR highlighting several inconsistencies with Nina Marshall's account of the shooting.

At the trial, Marshall reported seeing the two shooters at the foot of the bed firing guns wrapped in blankets or pillowcases. Yet there was no report of pillowcases discovered at the scene or observed in scene photographs. "The absence of singed and gunshot residue stain fibers from a gunshot through fabric is in conflict with Marshall's observation of pillowcase covered weapons during the discharge," according to the Knox report.[35]

The idea of gunshots muffled by pillowcases also conflicted with the statement of witnesses who reported the distinct sound of outside gunfire and would contradict the auditory experiments conducted at the scene by Knox & Associates.[36]

Marshall reported leaving the apartment approximately three minutes after the shooting when she said she saw Williams and Myers walking in the direction of the party at Rachel Jones's apartment. Detective Bowen said it took him only thirty to thirty-five seconds to walk from the scene to the back door of the party residence.

"In order for Marshall to have observed the shooters walking toward the party, she would have most likely made a hasty departure," the Knox report stated.[37]

Based on his review of the case, including crime scene reconstruction, gunfire experiments, and computer modeling, Knox offered the following conclusions in his independent report to the CIR:[38]

> It is most probable that the shots that struck the victims in this case were fired from outside the bedroom window, not from inside the bedroom.
>
> The wound path to the back of Jeanette Williams['s] head, coupled with the documented position of her body as depicted in the scene photographs, is consistent with the shot having come through the window, not from the foot of the bed.
>
> Gunfire testing indicates that it is unlikely that witnesses at a nearby party would have heard the gunfire if it was fired from inside the bedroom.
>
> The physical evidence in this case is consistent with shots having been fired from outside the bedroom window and into the bedroom.

Believing they had established the case for an outside shooter, the CIR zeroed in on another possible eyewitness to the shooting who could confirm their theory.

18

Eyewitness?

On July 13, 1976, police interviewed a man named Christopher Snype, who told them that his neighbor, Tony Gordon, said he witnessed the shooting two months earlier at the Morgan Street apartment. Gordon lived directly across the street from the victims.[1]

According to Snype, Gordon approached him and a friend, Major Skylark, around 4:00 a.m. on May 2, 1976, as they were sitting in Snype's mother's car. Gordon said he was in his living room when he heard the first shot fired, then looked out his window and saw a Black man in black clothing standing at the apartment window firing shots. The shooter then ran around to the back of the apartment. Gordon also told Snype that he went outside near the crime scene after the shooting and that when people found out that one person had died, Clifford Williams allegedly walked "over close to him, hit a car with his fist and said, '[expletive], one of the [expletive] ain't dead.'"[2]

After speaking with Snype, police interviewed Tony Gordon, who denied witnessing the shooting.

At the State's request, Gordon took a polygraph on July 14, 1976. During the prepolygraph interview, Gordon stated he had been sitting in his living room watching television in the early-morning hours of May 2 and could hear a party taking place down the street. He said he retired to his bedroom and heard what he thought to be gunshots. He stated that gunshots are very common in his neighborhood, and he did not get up to look out his window or take any other action. He admitted to going outside after the police arrived and said he watched Williams and Myers get arrested.[3]

Gordon said he knew Clifford "Boonie" Williams by sight and knew of his reputation but had never had any trouble with him. When asked to explain "Boonie's" reputation, he replied, "You know what I mean, if he wanted to get at you or your family, he could have done it."[4]

He also stated that everybody thinks "Boonie" knows somebody because "every time he has been arrested, he always gets out."[5]

Following the pretest interview, Gordon was asked the following questions as part of the polygraph exam:[6]

> Do you know for absolute sure who fired the shots at Baldie's window?
> After hearing the shots did you look outside and see a Black male running from Baldie's window?
> Did you tell anyone you saw a Black male run from Baldie's window?
> Did you tell anyone you heard "Boonie" say something like damn that other ***** ain't dead?"

The polygraphist concluded there was "significant deception" to the answers Gordon offered in responding to the questions. During the post-polygraph interview, Gordon was told his answers indicated he was being deceptive, and it was suggested that he had information concerning the homicide that could be beneficial if he would simply testify to what he had seen or heard. Gordon said there was no way he would testify because he had to "live on Morgan Street and he did not feel his family could be protected."[7]

He stated that if the jury turned "Boonie" loose, or even if they sent him away, someone could still get to his family.

"It is my opinion that Mr. Gordon did not tell me the truth during the polygraph examination and that his fear of reprisals concerning this incident are too great for him to take a chance and testify in this case," wrote polygraphist J. Donald Jones.[8]

It's a perspective that has long frustrated prosecutors, who often fail to secure an arraignment because of a potential witness's reluctance to come forward.

While Tony Gordon's name was made available to the defense team, nothing in the prosecution file indicates the defense counsel deposed Gordon or conducted any follow-up investigation.[9]

The prosecution did not list Christopher Snype or Major Skylark as witnesses, nor did it disclose Christopher Snype's written statement or the fact that Gordon failed a polygraph in pretrial discovery.[10] While the CIR does not directly state that evidence was withheld, the suppression by the prosecution of evidence favorable to the accused would violate due process (Brady v Maryland, 373 US 83, 87 (1963)).[11] (Brady requires the State to disclose material information within the State's possession or control that tends to negate the guilt of the defendant.)[12]

Both Snype and Skylark are since deceased.

More than four decades after the shooting, Tony Gordon was still living with his wife across the street from the 1550 Morgan Street apartment where the shooting took place. He was interviewed twice by the CIR investigative team. Despite the passage of time, Gordon made it clear he did not want to be involved. He again denied witnessing the shooting and told CIR investigators he had gotten to his current age by "minding his own business." He did offer that it was well known in the neighborhood that the damage to the window outside the 1550 Morgan Street apartment had occurred the night of the shooting.[13]

Did Gordon actually witness the shooting, as he allegedly told Snype and Skylark? And, if so, was the person he saw Nathaniel Lawson?

According to an affidavit, Lawson confessed to shooting Jeanette Williams and Nina Marshall from outside their apartment bedroom window. Tony Brown, a habitual offender and a close friend of Nathan Myers, signed the affidavit while in prison in 2014 outlining the details of Lawson's confession. Brown was interviewed by Thibodeau on a prison phone call on April 17, 2018. Brown told Thibodeau that Lawson had a bad reputation on the street for being dangerous and that he was confident that he was not the only one to whom Lawson would have admitted to the shootings.[14]

In addition to Brown, the CIR was able to identify and speak with three others to whom Lawson had allegedly confessed.

During the CIR investigation, Thibodeau was contacted by Ronald Stansell, the childhood friend of Nathan Myers. Hearing that the case was being reopened, Stansell provided Thibodeau the names and contact information of people who had mentioned over the years that Nathaniel Lawson had confessed to the shooting.[15]

Stansell said he first heard about Lawson's confession from Leatrice Carter, who said Lawson boasted he was the shooter when he visited her tavern sometime in the early 1990s.[16]

Stansell also provided contact information for James Stepps, the close friend of Lawson who said Lawson admitted to him he was the shooter shortly before his death in 1994.

Finally, the CIR interviewed Frank Williams, Clifford Williams's brother, who confronted Lawson about his role in the shooting and to whom Lawson allegedly confessed.

None of the witnesses to Lawson's confession sought any benefit from the information they provided to the CIR, according to Thibodeau.[17]

To connect the dots, Thibodeau and her team set out to confirm that Nathaniel Lawson was at or near the scene of the shooting on May 2, 1976.

The general offense report, filed the night of the shooting, noted that Detectives Bowen and Bradley observed a white pickup truck leaving the scene around the same time Myers and Williams were being transported to the Jacksonville Sheriff's Office. Police pulled the truck over so that it could be searched, according to the report. The driver was identified as Barbara Williams, the wife of Clifford Williams. One of the Black male passengers was identified as Raymond Rico Rivers. Two other passengers, one male and one female, were unidentified.[18]

In her 1976 deposition, Barbara Williams was asked:[19]

Q: "Who did you leave the party with when you left the area around 4:00 in the morning?"

A: "Rosetta Simmon [Cookie], Raymond [Rico Rivers] and Nathan Lawson."

Q: "Larson?"

A: "Lawson."

While Williams's deposition would seem to put Lawson at the scene, it does raise questions.

In his sworn affidavit detailing Lawson's confession, Tony Brown said: "Nathaniel [Lawson] told me that after he did the shooting, he ran and jump across the fence in the back of the apartment and ran to a car driven by Rico Rivers, who was parked waiting for him on Beaver Street. Nathaniel Lawson told me that Rico Rivers drove him to the Hilltop apartments, where they both stayed until the next day."[20]

If so, why, then, would both Lawson and Rivers still be at the scene in Barbara Williams's car two hours after the shooting?

"That was something we had raised," Thibodeau acknowledged. "Why would he [Nathaniel Lawson] have hung around a couple of hours in the vicinity? Was this something he cooked up with Rico Rivers . . . why didn't Nathaniel Lawson just run and get as far away as he could?

"I can't answer that."[21]

Rico Rivers was deposed by the prosecutor in 1976. He recalled arriving at Rachel Jones's party around 1:30 a.m. on May 2, 1976. After being at the party for fifteen to twenty minutes he remembered hearing four or five gunshots. At the time, he was standing in the kitchen eating, according to his deposition. His testimony was that Clifford Williams was also in the kitchen and that Nathan Myers was in the living room.[22]

This would seem to further contradict Nathaniel Lawson's claim to Tony Brown that immediately after the shooting he jumped into a waiting car driven by Rico Rivers.

The inconsistencies were neither ignored nor overlooked by the CIR team, according to Thibodeau.[23]

At the time of the CIR investigation, Rivers was residing in a nursing home. According to the nursing home staff, he suffered from dementia. Thibodeau attempted to speak with Rivers on three different occasions to try and get clarity on his activities the morning of the shooting but was unable to have a meaningful conversation.[24]

Another challenge of a case reopened after four decades.

19

Audit

By late November 2018, Shelley Thibodeau was getting restless.

"I felt like this was taking too much time," she recalled.[1]

It was a visit with Clifford Williams that added to her sense of urgency.

"We had waited to see Clifford until we were well into this investigation," Thibodeau said.

When Williams entered the interview room, he was weak and unstable, holding on to the wall for support.[2]

"I'm thinking, my God, this man is so frail, I don't think he's going to live much longer," Thibodeau said. "If we are going to do something, it has to get done, because what a shame it would be that it's November and we know what has to be done and he passes away in January."[3]

The CIR investigation had led to the following conclusions:

The shooting occurred from outside the bedroom window and not from inside. As such, it would have been physically impossible for Nina Marshall to have identified the shooter.

The trial strategy of failing to call witnesses or present evidence in order to preserve first and last closing arguments was not well reasoned given the plethora of witnesses and evidence available to the defense. As a result, the defendants were deprived of their right to a fair trial as contemplated by the United States Constitution.

Foregoing the forensics, the State relied on the testimony of one individual, the victim, in the face of overwhelmingly contradictory forensic evidence and alibi testimony. It was on this testimony alone that the two men had been convicted.

> A jury presented with the evidence known by the CIR could not
> conclude beyond a reasonable doubt that either defendant com-
> mitted the shooting and murder.[4]

As impatient as she was, Thibodeau said she understood that the process
had to run its course.

Other CIR units across the country had utilized an independent panel to
review their findings. She recommended to Melissa Nelson, who was being
kept apprised of the CIR's investigation, that they do the same in this case.

"I'd been a defense attorney for two decades and handled cases against
this office," Thibodeau said. "I thought it would be good for somebody independent to review what I'm doing so the Office, our law enforcement part-
ners, and the community understood that this wasn't just a defense attorney
trying to set someone free, but that this was somebody who was doing her
job to the best of her ability because I thought there was evidence to suggest
that somebody was innocent and had been wrongfully convicted and we
needed to rectify that situation."[5]

An independent audit board was convened, consisting of two former
prosecutors, a retired career public defender, a retired former FBI agent,
and a member of the Jacksonville business community.[6]

The audit board was supplied all the information and documentation
that was utilized by the CIR in issuing its report. The panel met on two
occasions to discuss the facts and circumstances surrounding the convictions.[7] The panel also heard from Hank Coxe, the prosecutor in the case,
who requested to address the panel. Exactly what he said to the panel was
never made public. However, it was later reported he told the panel he
agreed the men should be released and their convictions overturned. But,
calling the men absolutely innocent, he said, seemed a step too far.[8]

As part of its investigation, the CIR was able to locate the family of Jeanette "Baldie" Williams and discuss the case with them. Two of Jeanette's
sisters provided written statements, which were attached to the CIR report.

Joyce Young December 9, 2018
Subject: Clifford Williams and Nathan Myers

Jeanette Williams, no relation to Clifford Williams, was my sister who
as far back as I can remember was a caring and nurturing sister. She
looked after me and my nine siblings. She was our protector and on

May 2, 1976, she was taken away from us. Once a friend she was loyal to the end, a heart of gold and would not hurt a soul.

It is my understanding that those listed above proclaim their innocents [sic]. I feel that in my hearts of hearts they are not and if they didn't commit the crime, they played a part in it. As far as it goes, I forgive them for the final judgement will come from God. My heart continues to ache for the loss of my sister. My mother who is 89 years old still cries and gets depressed when talking about her and while life goes on, the pain continues to linger.

Sincerely, Joyce Young

Sharon A. Young
Re: Family of victim Jeannette [sic] E. Williams

Letter in reference to Clifford Williams, and Nathan Myers.

Feelings of forgiveness, first for the person/persons responsible for the Death of our loved one and my sister. It is my understanding that developments in the case has changed the original report and statements from witnesses. I am not sure if the developments will or not help the accused, I am sure that if one or both are innocent of the actual shooting, they are not innocent of coming forward before now when others claim to be guilty were alive, I ask the God we serve to punish those guilty of the crime and forgive the innocent if there are any.

I forgive, but I will never forget the pain and sorrow of the tragic death of my sister and those involved, rather [sic] they pulled the trigger or had knowledge of who did or ordered it, they are just as guilty. What I am also sure of is the one responsible will pay for their crime if not while living in death. I close with the fact my Mother lost a child, we lost a sister, and others lost a relative and a friend, how do you replace that. . . .

May God have mercy on the guilty and innocent.

Respectfully Submitted, Sharon A. Young

The CIR was unable to locate the family of Nina Marshall.

After their review of the full CIR report and discussions, the independent audit board unanimously concluded there was not sufficient evidence of guilt to support the convictions of Nathan Myers and Clifford Williams.

And although there was no definitive proof of innocence, such as DNA evidence, the panel agreed there was sufficient evidence to support a finding that they were, in fact, "probably" innocent of the charges.[9]

Having concluded all its investigative work, the CIR signed off on its final report on February 25, 2019, recommending to State Attorney Melissa Nelson that a determination be made that the office "has lost faith" in the convictions of both Nathan Myers and Clifford Williams.[10]

"While no single item of evidence in and of itself exonerates defendant Myers or defendant Williams, the culmination of all the evidence, most of which the jury never heard or saw, leaves no abiding confidence in their convictions or the guilt of the defendants," the CIR concluded.[11]

The CIR report determined, "There is no credible evidence of guilt, and likewise there is credible evidence of innocence. These men would not be convicted by a jury in 2019 if the jury were presented with all the exculpatory evidence."[12]

The report recommended the State Attorney's Office support efforts to vacate the convictions of both Myers and Williams, and if granted by the court, dismiss the indictments rendered against them more than four decades ago.[13]

The prospects for freedom, faint for so long, were now within a court's earshot.

20

Free at Last

"Don't die on me now," Nathan Myers pleaded with his uncle. "We've come this far."[1]

With the possibility of their freedom seemingly imminent, Myers was rightfully concerned about the health of his uncle Clifford. Williams appeared weak, frail, and unsteady, requiring a walker for balance. He was vomiting, which prison officials attributed to some bad mayonnaise.[2]

But Myers sensed his uncle's health had been deteriorating for months. What no one knew at the time was that Williams was suffering from an advanced case of prostate cancer, which had gone undetected in prison.

Myers encouraged his uncle to hold on. "God is going to give us another chance," he said.[3]

With the CIR having filed its final report on the investigation, things began moving at a rapid pace toward exoneration. But there were still some obstacles to overcome.

There was no mechanism in Florida for the State Attorney's Office to file a motion to vacate a prison sentence. There were some potential options such as filing a motion based on "manifest injustice."

"We decided that because this was so important and we had the desire to get this done, that this was maybe not a good time to try and make these novel arguments," Thibodeau said.[4]

Instead, she enlisted the help of the Innocence Project of Florida and the law firm Holland & Knight to file motions before the court. Both firms were familiar with the case. The Innocence Project of Florida filed a motion on behalf of Nathan Myers that his sentence be vacated based in large measure on the findings of the CIR unit. Holland & Knight adopted the motion on behalf of Clifford Williams, whom they represented pro bono.

"As demonstrated *supra,* the CIR report stands on its own as newly discovered evidence. . . . Had this evidence been available at the time of his
trial, a jury probably would have acquitted," the motion read.[5]

As part of its legal foundation, the motion cited Jones v. State 591 So. 2d
911, 915-16 (Fla. 1991), which held that to be eligible for relief, the defendant must proffer "newly discovered evidence [that is] of such a nature that
it would probably produce an acquittal on retrial."[6]

The motion to vacate asked the court to dismiss all indictments against
the two men and that they be immediately released from state custody. A
hearing was set for March 28, 2019, in front of Circuit Court Judge Angela
M. Cox.

When he woke up the morning of the hearing, Nathan Myers said, his
heart was racing.

He skipped breakfast. He prayed and reflected.

"I was just so overwhelmed that I might be going home," he said.[7]

Overcome with joy, his emotions were tempered.

"I kept wondering who would be there." He knew his wife Rose would
be waiting for him.[8]

"My momma, my daddy, my brother, my sister, my grandmamma, my
grandaddy, all of them were gone," he reflected. "Maybe, a few years earlier
some of them would have seen me get out."[9]

Myers arrived at the Duval County courthouse on March 28, 2019, with
a small bag of clothes he brought from the Sumter County jail. As he waited
in a holding cell with his uncle, he was provided with a dress suit by his
social worker. For Myers, it was the fulfillment of a prophecy.

Ernest Edwards, chief investigator for the CIR, had told Myers on more
than one occasion during the investigation, "You are going home. What
size suit do you wear? You are going to need a suit to talk at the podium."[10]

At the morning hearing, Judge Cox acted decisively. She spoke of the
challenges of reviewing the entire case history dating back to May 1976 and
stated she was only three years old when the two men had been arrested.
She praised all the attorneys who had worked on the case from the very
beginning until the present, saying they were "brilliant legal minds in this
community, leaders in this community."[11]

Before issuing her order, she asked if there was anyone at the hearing
representing the victim, Jeanette Williams. There was no one present on
her behalf.

Judge Cox then restated the key findings of the CIR report and concluded that "justice demands granting these motions" that the sentences for both men be vacated.[12]

Shelley Thibodeau, seated next to State Attorney Melissa Nelson, then addressed the court:

"The State is not aware of any credible evidence that would sustain a finding of guilt in this case and for that reason, at this time the State of Florida dismisses the indictments that were returned against Mr. Williams and Mr. Myers."[13]

Judge Cox responded, "Mr. Williams and Mr. Myers, the indictments have been dismissed against you. You are free to go."[14]

Those words brought a sudden and emotional end to a forty-three-year fight for justice for Myers and Williams. Myers rose and hugged his legal team. Williams remained seated and wept. The two men then quietly embraced each other as attorneys, courtroom officials, and family members looked on in silent reverence. There was a tearful reuniting of families in the courtroom including Williams's three grown children, his brother Frank, and several family friends.

A celebratory lunch was held with the families, attorneys, and others involved with the case.

The two freed men, accompanied by their supporters, were then led out the door of the State Attorney's Office into the bright Florida sunshine, where a sea of media awaited.

Both men pointed skyward, praising God.

Myers gingerly bent over, cleaned off a patch of the brick sidewalk, knelt to both knees, and kissed the ground.

"Praise the Lord!" "Hallelujah!" "Free at Last!" echoed the crowd of supporters.

Myers told reporters the notion of "freedom" had not yet registered.

"It's nerve-wracking right now," he said. "I'm nervous because I feel like I'm still locked up."[15]

A weeping Williams, with a Bible in front of him, said, "My mother died while I was on death row. I just wanted to get out to see my kids."[16]

State Attorney Melissa Nelson called it a "historic day." The exoneration had validated her early commitment to establish Florida's first CIR unit.

"We have a continuing post-conviction ethical obligation to pursue justice when we become aware of material evidence suggesting a conviction is not correct," she said, adding that "putting justice above all else" is rooted in that obligation.[17]

In a press conference after the court's ruling, the first person Nelson thanked was Hank Coxe, the former prosecutor, who along with attorney Buddy Schulz, had been the catalyst for convincing her of the need for a CIR unit in Jacksonville.

"If not for Hank and Buddy, this unit would not be a reality," she acknowledged, without reference to the irony of Coxe being the original prosecutor for the case that had just been dismissed.[18]

For Shelley Thibodeau, the exoneration was both a legal and personal victory. During the course of the CIR investigation, she had become convinced that the two men were innocent. As the new evidence emerged, she acknowledged being consumed with getting the men out of prison. Yet she felt the need to cover every detail because she knew there would be questions, even within her own office, where the idea of a CIR unit had not been fully embraced.

The internal resistance seemed to emanate not so much from the effort to correct a wrongful conviction, but more from the fact that this specific case centered around Clifford "Boonie" Williams, whose reputation among law enforcement was that of a hardened criminal.

"I know there were people who were not happy we were looking at the case," said Jim McMillan, director of the State Attorney's Trial Services division, whose work was a major component of the CIR report. "There were people who were not happy we had started this unit to begin with."[19]

Aside from the CIR team, there were only a few representatives from the State Attorney's Office present at the program held inside the office's ceremonial courtroom the day of the exoneration.

Disappointed, McMillan sent an office-wide email that said those who didn't come "missed an historic occasion."[20]

Outside, Nathan Myers climbed into a car with his wife, Rose, and her grandson. Nathan and Rose had been married since 2005 but had never spent a night together outside of prison.

As they headed to Rose's Orlando home, Nathan kept looking out his back window.

"I kept looking back, making sure we weren't going to be pulled over by the police and have to go back," he recalled. "I did that all the way to Orlando."[21]

21

Beware of the Stare

Now fully exonerated, Myers quickly discovered that "feeling free" was a different matter. His worry that the police might come back after him lingered. It's a sentiment shared by other exonerees.

Keith Harward, exonerated in Virginia in 2016 after spending thirty-three years in prison for a murder he did not commit, had his story profiled on the popular true-crime podcast *Criminal*.

When asked by the show's moderator, Phoebe Judge, "What was it like when you walked out of prison a free man?" Harward responded: "Well, I'm not free. I'll never be free. I'm un-incarcerated."[1]

"Everybody knows I didn't do it," Harward continued, "but you know you can't help but think, wow, what could they do to me again? There's no freedom to that. I'm just not incarcerated. It's always a great day not to be in prison but as far as a free thing, let there be no doubt 'til the day I drop, it will be with me."[2]

In Myers's case, he could not escape the sense that people were staring at him. Whether sitting on his front porch or going to the grocery store, Myers was leery.

"Staring is a no-no in prison," he said with conviction. It was a sure sign that trouble was on the way.[3]

"I was paranoid," Myers admitted. "Wherever I was, I felt like people were staring at me."[4]

His exoneration had generated headlines and extensive press coverage. His newfound celebrity made him recognizable to some. In other cases, his imagination and paranoia may have gotten the best of him.

It was one of the many adjustments the sixty-one-year-old would have to make after spending almost all his adult life in jail.

"The world had changed a whole lot," Myers said. "I didn't know nothing about Facebook, Instagram, none of that stuff. I did learn how to text and, as long as I could dial a number, I was going to be OK."[5]

He remembered how to drive, but it took more than one attempt to pass his driver's test. He had to meet with Social Security and find his way back into society with little, if any, financial resources.

He settled in with his wife, Rose, in her small home in Orlando on South Cottage Hill Road. He kept his activities to a minimum, visiting with family and practicing his faith.

When he did venture out, he was cautious.

"My wife and I went to the grocery store, and we were pushing a buggy," Myers recalled. "She had put her purse in the front part with the zipper open. I told her to put her purse in the bottom of the buggy because people might be looking around thinking I'm trying to put stuff in that purse."[6]

A highlight for Myers was attending his first live football game after his release. Living only a few blocks away from Camping World Stadium, Myers walked over to watch the Florida Gators defeat the Miami Hurricanes to open the 2019 college football season. A Gators fan, Myers still retained a critical eye for football strategy and technique.

For Clifford Williams, his first days of freedom were spent with his daughter and attending to his deteriorating medical condition. Within weeks of his release, he was diagnosed with an aggressive prostate cancer that had gone undetected in prison. For almost two months, he underwent daily radiation treatment at the University of Florida Health Proton Institute in Jacksonville. The ultramodern, high-tech proton beam therapy was quite the contrast to anything Williams had ever seen on death row or within the walls of the Florida prison system.

There is a tradition at the Proton Institute that patients ring a celebratory bell at the end of their treatment regimen. For Williams, the ringing of the bell represented yet another kind of freedom.

"When they said the words 'cancer free,' all I could do was praise God," he said.[7]

Not long after his release, Williams married Leatrice Carter, his friend from childhood. Carter was among those to whom Nathaniel Lawson had allegedly confessed about the murder of Jeanette Williams.

Like his nephew, Williams kept his postexoneration activities to a minimum, going to church and spending time with family. The temptations of a previous lifestyle seemed like a distant memory.

"We're about to get married," Leatrice Carter proclaimed. "He can't do that no more."[8]

While the two exonerees were adjusting to life outside of prison, their story and the work of Florida's first Conviction Integrity Review (CIR) unit was receiving a healthy dose of national media attention. The story was covered by CNN, NBC, the *New York Times,* and other major news outlets. It was featured on the popular podcast *Criminal* in an episode titled "The Night of the Party."

Most of the coverage was positive, hailing the achievements of the CIR unit and praising the leadership of State Attorney Melissa Nelson.

"It's never too late to do the right thing," stated an editorial in the *Florida Times-Union.* "State Attorney Melissa Nelson deserves credit and praise for establishing the CIR unit and for providing the backing that has allowed it to get off to such a good start."[9]

The *Times-Union* editorial continued that such a unit would have been "unthinkable" under Nelson's predecessor, Angela Corey.[10] (Corey's supporters might have disagreed, conjecturing she wouldn't have needed a special unit to seek an exoneration of someone wrongfully convicted.)

Not everyone was so convinced about the outcome of the CIR investigation.

John Delaney is the former mayor of Jacksonville and was assistant state attorney under Ed Austin in the early 1980s. On July 7, 2019, Delaney penned a lengthy op-ed piece in the *Florida Times-Union* critical of the exoneration and the media hoopla surrounding it.

"The case was fairly tried by competent defense lawyers and a fair judge," Delaney wrote. "Jurors, judges and justices found that Williams committed that murder based on the victim's testimony. . . . A completely neutral Florida Supreme Court confirmed the conviction. Now, Williams walks a free man with the media declaring him to be innocent."[11]

"Efforts to clear the innocent are noble," Delaney wrote. But with respect to Williams and Myers, prosecutors and police from the era "recall a different case than the one the media described."[12]

Delaney hearkened back to another case from the 1970s in which boxer Rubin "Hurricane" Carter was sentenced to life in prison for a triple murder in Patterson, New Jersey. The case took on additional national prominence when Bob Dylan wrote a popular song proclaiming that the witnesses lied and that Carter had been falsely tried. Carter was eventually released.

"Many think Hurricane Carter, while given two unfair trials, was indeed guilty as absolute hell," Delaney wrote.[13]

Citing a line in the Dylan song that the media "all went along for the ride" in originally accusing Carter, Delaney opined the same happened with the media in the Williams-Myers case, "this time in condemning the lawyers and the judge as corrupt, incompetent, or biased. Such was hardly the case."[14]

Delaney defended the defense attorney's strategy of not calling any witnesses in order to have the last word before the jury, saying that a cross-examination of the alibi witnesses of "dubious credibility" was more likely to hurt Williams's case than help it.

He wrote that Williams could have testified in his own behalf but refused to "at the one time when it really would have mattered. . . . As with the alleged alibi witnesses, Williams and his lawyer consciously decided not to put Williams on the stand."[15]

In the op-ed piece, Delaney placed little credibility in the alleged confession of Nathaniel Lawson.

"As occurs in tough crime-laden neighborhoods, perhaps a thug wanting a reputation whispers that he is the actual killer," Delaney wrote. "In this case a drug dealing thug without a known motive and apparently no other evidence to implicate him. As tantalizing as this seems now, if all it takes to beat a murder rap is for someone else across town to unprovably confess to it, we will have a lot of such confessions. And lots of beaten murder raps."[16]

Delaney's op-ed piece set off a war of words with the city's longtime public defender Bill White, since retired, who served on the CIR's independent audit committee.

White responded with his own op-ed piece the following week, calling Delaney's suggestions "uninformed and reckless."[17]

"Unlike Delaney, I saw all of the evidence that led to the board's unanimous conclusion," White wrote. "I want to believe that had Delaney first asked to review the evidence he would not have made such reckless and uninformed suggestions. . . . There is a danger in having someone like Delaney disparage alibi witnesses whose statements he has not read."[18]

White defended the findings of the CIR, writing that, "Viewing evidence now that was never presented to a jury makes it clear beyond any doubt that the shots were fired from outside and not inside. . . . Techniques that were not generally in use when the case was tried but that are standard police practice today confirmed a finding that the shooting could not have happened as the eyewitness victim testified."[19]

White concluded, "I've known John Delaney for over 30 years. I knew he was, as am I, a fan of Bob Dylan. But to write that 'many people' still think Hurricane Carter was guilty or that somehow 'the media all went along for the ride' . . . is to make an argument that is based on non-sequiturs."[20]

Inside the State Attorney's Office there continued to be rumblings about the CIR and the exoneration of Myers and Williams. Some questioned how the investigation was handled and cringed at the publicity Williams was receiving, given his prior criminal background.

Jim McMillan, the forensic artist who played a major role in the CIR investigation, drew individual portraits of Myers and Williams that were initially displayed prominently in the hallway of the State Attorney's Office. It did not sit well for some, especially for those familiar with Williams's criminal past. The portraits were taken down and moved into Shelley Thibodeau's office.

Hank Coxe, the original prosecutor in the case and the catalyst for the creation of the CIR, weighed in on the exoneration shortly after the two men were released.

"Are they possibly innocent, I'd say sure they're possibly innocent," Coxe told Corley Peel of News Jax4 in a television interview. "Do I think what the State Attorney's Office put together is a product that points to innocence? I'm not that comfortable it does. I think it does point to the lack of integrity of how the conviction resulted."[21]

As the public discourse continued, Coxe's daughter, Katie Coxe Fackler, also an attorney, offered a conciliatory and personal message with her own letter to the editor in the *Florida Times-Union* on April 2, 2019:[22]

After the *Times-Union* published its third article about the recently overturned convictions of Nathan Myers and Clifford Williams, my mom sent the following text to me and my siblings:

"Your dad and I have always believed the maxim that it is better for 100 guilty men to go free than for one innocent man to be incarcerated. Two down, 98 to go."

My dad is Hank Coxe, the prosecutor in the Myers and Williams cases; my mom, Mary Coxe, then a prosecutor herself, lived through their trials.

Ironically, my parents were instrumental in Melissa Nelson's successful campaign for State Attorney in 2016; my dad was equally supportive of the establishment of the state attorney's conviction integrity unit.

Nelson—and that unit—have just told him that he got it wrong.

My mother's response epitomizes the attitudes of forgiveness, understanding and reconciliation we need so desperately in our current political climate.

My parents continue to seek to be a part of what is right and just, setting aside their personal feelings for the betterment of our society. May we all do the same.

Two down, 98 to go.

Katie Coxe Fackler

22

Clean Hands

In 2008, Florida passed a wrongful conviction compensation law that provides exonerees fifty thousand dollars for each year served as a result of a wrongful incarceration. However, the law included a restriction that those with a prior felony conviction for unrelated crimes are not eligible for the compensation.

Critics say this "clean hands" restriction ultimately bars most exonerees from collecting any funds after their release, since most have a prior criminal record.[1] Indeed, only ten of the seventy-seven current exonerees in Florida have ever received compensation under the law, according to the University of Michigan's National Registry of Exonerations.[2]

Of thirty-seven states with wrongful conviction compensation laws, Florida is the only one with a "clean hands" restriction. Numerous attempts in the Florida Legislature to remove the "clean hands" provision have fallen short.

"Despite all that exonerees went through during their wrongful incarcerations the injustice continues after exoneration for those unfairly excluded from compensation," wrote Seth Miller, executive director of the Innocence Project of Florida, in an op-ed piece in the *Florida Times-Union*. "This bar is particularly unfair because having a prior criminal record makes a person more likely to be wrongfully convicted in the first place."[3]

For Clifford Williams and Nathan Myers, Florida's compensation law had particular consequences. Both were convicted and ultimately exonerated for the same crime. Yet, because Williams had two prior felony convictions when he was age eighteen and twenty-three, he was ineligible for any compensation under the law despite having served a full forty-two years in prison (including a stint on death row) for a crime he was judged not to have committed.

Myers, meanwhile, was eligible for the compensation, capped at $2 million, because he had no prior felony convictions.

The Myers-Williams case and the issue of compensation got the attention of the 2020 Florida Legislature.

A special claims bill was filed on behalf of Williams in both arms of the Florida Legislature asking that he be compensated for his time in prison. While the state law made him ineligible based on his prior felony convictions, the legislature was not bound by that restriction and had the authority to pass a special claims bill in support of Williams.

Senate Bill 28 was filed by Senate Minority Leader Audrey Gibson, a Jacksonville Democrat, while House Bill 6507 was filed on behalf of Williams by Jacksonville Democrat Kimberly Daniels.

A special master was assigned for each bill to file a report and make a recommendation.

A series of hearings and interviews were conducted that included CIR director Shelley Thibodeau. She was pressed on the issue of possible motives for the shooting, including Nina Marshall's allegation that she overheard a conversation that Williams and Myers may have been involved in another murder and that they buried the victim in the woods.

(The brother of the victim told Thibodeau that he heard someone other than Williams and Myers had been responsible for the death.)[4]

"The CIR director was unable to substantiate any of the alleged potential motives," according to the Senate's "Special Master's Final Report," submitted by Christie M. Letarte.[5]

In their final reports to their respective houses of the Florida Legislature, both special masters recommended approval of the claims bill.

"Because Claimant has demonstrated by clear and convincing evidence that he is actually innocent of the crimes for which he was convicted in 1976, I recommend that House Bill 6507 be reported FAVORABLY," wrote W. Jordan Jones, House of Representatives special master.[6]

The special claims bill sailed through committees with uncharacteristic bipartisan support.

Legislators in both parties used the hearings to point out flaws in the justice system and to apologize to Williams for how he had been treated.

"It's never too late for justice," said Rep. Paul Renner, chairman of the Florida House Judiciary Committee. "We're sorry it's taken this long."[7]

Williams's daughter, Tracy Williams-Magwood, addressed the House Judiciary Committee on February 26, 2020, recalling her visits to her father on death row when she was just four years old. She told committee members her mother had died during childbirth.

"My father to me, was more of a father than some outside the prison walls," she said.[8]

While the Williamses' claim bill was being favorably reviewed, there was yet another surprise about to unfold in this tangled saga. Because Nathan Myers had no previous convictions, his petition for compensation under Florida's Victims of Wrongful Incarceration Compensation Act seemed a foregone conclusion. Under the law, Myers qualified for the $2 million cap.

However, on January 23, 2020, the Florida Attorney General's Office, under Ashley Moody, determined that Myers's application did not meet the standard for compensation, effectively denying his petition for compensation.

The opinion, authored by Associate Deputy Attorney General Carolyn Snurkowski, stated that Myers had not proven his innocence.

"Although Mr. Myers' convictions and sentences have been vacated, the Department cannot conclude that Mr. Myers is innocent or that such a finding has been established," Snurkowski wrote in a letter to the Innocence Project of Florida, who was representing Myers.[9]

Snurkowski noted the compensation statute requires that a petitioner "prove by clear and convincing evidence" that he is factually innocent.[10]

"Therefore, to receive compensation, Myers must prove it is highly probable that he is factually innocent of the murder and attempted murder for which he was convicted," she wrote.[11]

Snurkowski's January 23 letter initially received no public attention in a case that had been highly publicized.

Weeks later, on Friday evening, February 14, news broke on a local television station that Myers's petition had been denied by the Attorney General's Office.

The next morning, headlines on the front page of the *Florida Times-Union* read:

Wrongful Conviction; No Reparations.

That same morning, in a sudden reversal, the Attorney General's Office determined that Snurkowski had overstepped her bounds by second-guessing decisions made by the courts in either vacating a conviction or determining that a petitioner was wrongfully incarcerated and eligible for compensation.[12]

Snurkowski's role was limited to simply reviewing the application to ensure it contained all the materials required by the State, according to the Attorney General's Office.

"As the statute does not permit the DLA [Department of Legal Affairs] to reject an application due to procedural or evidentiary concerns with a court finding, the DLA will inform the Chief Financial Officer that the application meets the requirements of the statute and is complete," wrote Richard H. Martin, general counsel for the Florida Department of Legal Affairs.[13]

It was another roller-coaster ride for Nathan Myers, who cleared the final hurdle on his way to freedom and compensation for time served.

Clifford Williams's claim bill received unanimous bipartisan support in both houses of the Florida Legislature.

Ironically, by proceeding outside the state law, the Williams claims bill was not subject to the $2 million cap. The final bill before the Florida Legislature asked that Williams be compensated at $2.15 million, based on the statutory amount of $50,000 for each year served. An amendment provided that the compensation be handled through an irrevocable trust as opposed to an annuity, making access to the funds more readily available for Williams, subject to the approval of three appointed cotrustees.

As the claims bill passed unanimously in the Republican-controlled Florida Senate, legislators rose to a standing ovation for Williams as he looked on with his family from the public gallery. He had come a long way in his journey from being a drug-dealing kingpin who spent more than fifty years of his life in prison, including time on death row for the Morgan Street murder.

Efforts to remove the "clean hands" restriction from the Florida statute, which seemed to have gained momentum as a result of the Myers-Williams exoneration, failed to make it to the finish line in the 2020 legislative session, despite having passed six committees. Advocates for removing the "clean hands" provision vowed to press on.

Florida governor Ron DeSantis signed Williams's Special Claims Bill on June 9, 2020.

For Clifford "Boonie" Williams and Nathan Myers, justice had at long last been achieved.

23

Epilogue

On a sunny day, September 19, 2021, Nathan and Rose Myers walked into the God Is Able Outreach Ministry in Orlando dressed in all white with matching KN95 masks.

The COVID-19 precautions could not cover up or hide the joy on their faces on this special day.

Inside the church both Nathan and Rose were conferred their Certificates of Ordination as Deacons of the Ministry. It was a jubilant and spiritual moment, the culmination of diligent study and commitment to their faith and to each other.

After receiving a portion of his wrongful conviction proceeds, Nathan and Rose settled into a modest home, tastefully decorated, in a gated Orlando community. A corner hall is dedicated to press clippings chronicling his life's journey. His freedom from financial worries has done little to change his simple, postexoneration lifestyle. Faith and family have remained his priorities. His attempt to work as a mentor to juveniles in the criminal justice system has been delayed in a sea of bureaucracy and background checks.[1] He has spoken to some youth and church groups as well as civic organizations, and he accompanied Melissa Nelson and Shelley Thibodeau on a trip to Baltimore to address a group of judges and prosecutors. It was his first time on an airplane.

"I was scared to death," he recalled.[2]

He has since flown again, this time to Arizona to a retreat with other exonerated defendants sponsored by the Innocence Project.

His uncle Clifford moved to a rural setting in North Florida with his wife, Leatrice. Clifford's outings are mostly limited to doctor visits, according to Myers. They see little of each other these days.

Florida's first Conviction Integrity Review (CIR) unit continues its mission in the Fourth Judicial Circuit. More than four years into its existence, the Myers-Williams case remains its only exoneration, although others are potentially in the works.

The unit reviews around thirty to thirty-five cases a year. Exonerations are not the only measure of success. In researching a recent petition, new DNA evidence reaffirmed a defendant's conviction.

"They got it right," said Shelley Thibodeau. "I consider that a win, too."[3]

The Jacksonville-based CIR did play a role in assisting with what would become a controversial exoneration of Edward Clayton Taylor, convicted of raping a four-year-old child in 1986. The case of mistaken identity was initially handled by the Innocence Project of Florida, which succeeded in having Taylor's 1987 conviction vacated in 2022, three years after he had been paroled when his accuser acknowledged to the Florida Parole Commission she had mistakenly identified Taylor as her attacker. This, in addition to other evidence, led the CIR to recommend the State not oppose Taylor's motion for postconviction relief in a hearing in May 2022.[4]

Only a month after his case was officially vacated as a wrongful conviction, Taylor was arrested in Jacksonville on charges of attempted murder. The Jacksonville Sheriff's Office Real-Time Crime Camera captured the shooting on video.

Shortly after the arrest, the Innocence Project of Florida released a statement standing by the exoneration of the rape charges and said that after the case was vacated, they no longer represented Taylor.

"The collaborative effort to both free and vacate the wrongful conviction of Edward Taylor required years of painstaking, diligent and thorough investigation by state and defense entities. We stand by that work and result. We cannot predict the future and our focus at the Innocence Project of Florida is squarely on freeing the wrongfully convicted because that is what justice demands. With the end of the postconviction process, so too ended our representation of Mr. Taylor."[5]

The CIR unit also defended its position with regard to the exoneration and said the State Attorney's Office would conduct an investigation of the new attempted-murder charge.

"In the three years since his release, the CIR thoroughly investigated the matter and discovered evidence that had not been disclosed to Taylor's defense. This failure, in conjunction with other errors and the victim's recantation, informed the State's decision to consent to Taylor's post-conviction motion. We stand by the CIR's work in that case. As in all cases, the State will review Taylor's unrelated arrest and make a filing decision."[6]

At his arraignment, Taylor entered a "Not Guilty" plea to the upgraded charge of second-degree murder.

The State Attorney's Office in the Fourth Judicial Circuit, under Melissa Nelson's leadership, continues to receive high marks in its successful prosecution rate and community partnerships such as its restorative justice initiative and its Mental Health Offender Program.

In its 2021 Annual Report, the State Attorney's Office noted a 30 percent reduction in murders and a 17 percent reduction in shootings from the prior year.

"We believe this significant decline has been achieved, in part, through policy changes, novel prosecutions, partnerships and investment in technology," the report states. (The murder rate has increased again since that report.)

Conviction Integrity Units have now been established in four other Florida judicial circuits: Hillsborough, Broward, Palm Beach, Orange, and Osceola Counties.

On September 14, 2020, the murder and rape conviction of Robert DuBoise was vacated in Hillsborough County, Florida, due in part to the collaborative efforts of the Innocence Project of Florida and the CIR unit established in the Thirteenth Judicial Circuit by State Attorney Andrew Warren. DNA testing of old evidence excluded DuBoise, who was convicted based on a bite mark that evidence suggested never happened in the first place.[7]

Much like Clifford Williams, DuBoise spent time on death row during his thirty-seven years in prison. And, like Williams, because of prior convictions, he was not entitled to compensation for his time spent in jail under the "clean hands" provision of Florida's wrongful conviction statute. A claims bill was filed on his behalf in the 2022 Florida Legislature seeking $1.85 million.

"He spent decades on Death Row because of questionable evidence presented by the State," said state Senator Jeff Brandes, a St. Petersburg Republican sponsoring DuBoise's claim bill. "If anyone thinks justice was served simply by releasing him without compensating him that's not justice. Just letting him out is not justice."[8]

On Monday, March 13, 2023, Sidney Holmes was exonerated after serving thirty-four years for a 1988 Broward County armed robbery he did not commit. This came as a result of a collaborative reinvestigation of the case by the Innocence Project of Florida and the Broward County Conviction Review Unit.

The Florida examples are only a microcosm of the national crisis of wrongful convictions and the growing trend among prosecutors to recognize their own role in seeking justice on all fronts, not just in the number of convictions.

This trend has resulted in a proliferation of Conviction Integrity Units (CIUs) within prosecutorial offices nationwide. Since 2002, more than ninety CIUs have been established.[9]

"Several Conviction Integrity Units have accomplished a great deal in a short period of time, and there has certainly been an uptick in the number of offices that claim to have formed CIUs. It is still too soon to know whether this trend will produce a change in the way prosecutors operate generally," reads the National Registry's website.[10]

Diverse in nature, the various Conviction Integrity Units operate under their own set of guidelines with no universally adopted set of standards or practices. Yet their emergence represents a powerful paradigm shift from the more traditional route of pro bono defense attorneys working to overturn wrongful convictions.

"In short, there is a fundamental and important difference between the kind of granular, deep dives into problematic cases that inevitably occur in a good non-adversarial CIU investigation, and the adversarial post-conviction review pursued on appeal or collateral attack," writes Barry Scheck, cofounder of the Innocence Project.[11]

While mostly praised by the legal community, the units are not without controversy.

The Baltimore, Maryland, CIU, under the direction of former state attorney Marilyn Mosby, won exonerations for nine people since she took office in 2015. But the unit has come under criticism by some former prosecutors and police officers who consider it a rebuke of their work.[12]

After three Black men were exonerated for the 1987 murder of a fellow middle school student, the lead detective on the case, Donald Kincaid, accused Mosby of trying to make the police "look like liars and cheats."[13]

Mosby has since been indicted on federal charges of perjury and making false mortgage applications related to the purchase of a vacation home in Florida. She was defeated in her party's primary in her bid for reelection in 2022.

While Conviction Integrity Units are growing in popularity, some question their effectiveness. More than half of the established units have yet to record an exoneration.[14] This has raised the issue of whether funding these units is the best use of otherwise scarce resources.

For those wrongfully convicted, whose options have seemingly been exhausted, the Conviction Integrity Units are a lifeline.

"When a person goes into court, they are presumed innocent," said Jim McMillan. "But if they are found guilty and that guilty verdict is shown to be unsubstantiated, they don't get that presumed innocence again. They're presumed guilty . . . and it's much harder to get somebody out of prison for whom you have evidence of their innocence, than it is to get somebody into prison."[15]

McMillan said that was just one of the revelations that came to him from his work on the Myers-Williams case.

"I was shocked and saddened that not only did this happen, but by my discovery that this happens a lot more than people think that it does," he said.[16]

The National Registry of Exonerations keeps a running tab. In its June 2021 report titled *25,000 Years Lost to Wrongful Convictions,* the Registry acknowledged that its counts are low.

"The vast majority of false convictions go uncorrected and therefore are never counted," according to the report.[17]

While calling the staggering number of years lost a "dark milestone," it only begins to tell the story of wrongful convictions and the toll they take, according to the report.[18]

"For people wrongfully incarcerated, every year is a lost year," the report reads. "To exonerees who served sentences of a year or two for crimes they did not commit, it must have felt like an eternity. For those who served decades, the suffering is incomprehensible."[19]

The exoneration of Nathan Myers and Clifford Williams, which was featured in the Registry's 2021 report, had its share of twists and turns, demonstrating the complexity of these cases, often decades old. Many of the key figures, including the victims, witnesses, and attorneys, were deceased. Having a seasoned defense attorney with no prosecutorial experience working inside the Prosecutor's Office and leading the reinvestigation was bound to raise questions. And in this instance, the irony of having the community's catalyst for a Conviction Integrity Unit having his own case vacated by the very unit he helped establish cannot be understated.

At a 2022 Federal Bar Association Jacksonville Chapter awards presentation, State Attorney Nelson acknowledged the delicate balance required with a Conviction Integrity Unit in her office.

"I concede that exonerations, and publicity around exonerations, may make seeking a conviction tougher," Nelson said. "But our community exacting high standards on the system . . . does not mitigate our obligation to pursue justice. I also believe that our willingness to audit our work, own our mistakes and use them for the sake of good should build trust in the system."[20]

Distinguishing between "wrongfully convicted" and "factually innocent" presents another challenge for prosecutors and Conviction Integrity Units. In a justice system that strives to balance the scales, there will continue to be innocent people in jail and guilty ones on the street.

What is clear, is that Florida's first CIR unit helped secure the freedom for Nathan Myers and Clifford Williams that had otherwise been unattainable for more than four decades.

"Without them, we would have died in prison, for sure," Myers said.[21]

Myers believes there are many others like him, in prison for a crime they didn't commit.

His advice, which he said applies to life, is simple.

"Don't ever give up," he said. "Once you give up on yourself, you are doomed."[22]

And, as his own case proved, it's never too late.

Acknowledgments

Writing about a story that spans more than four decades requires the cooperation and support of many.

At the top of this list are the two exonerees, Nathan Myers and Clifford Williams. Their willingness to speak openly about the case, including their early lives and events leading up to their arrest for murder, was a critical element in the retelling of this story. Myers's vivid recollections of the trial, his years in prison, and his postconviction adjustment to the outside world added a personal perspective to the legal maneuverings.

This book would not have been possible without the assistance of the State Attorney's Office (SAO) of the Fourth Judicial Circuit in Florida. The author is especially grateful to State Attorney Melissa Nelson and to the Conviction Integrity Review (CIR) Director Shelley Thibodeau for giving their time, perspective, and access to documents and photographs. The author would also like to thank Jim McMillan and Tom Brady of the SAO for their valuable contributions.

Perhaps no one had a more unique role in this story than attorney Hank Coxe, the original prosecutor who years later was a catalyst for the establishment of a CIR unit in the Fourth Judicial Circuit. Much gratitude and appreciation to Hank for his full cooperation and perspective. Attorney Buddy Schulz, who along with Coxe was a major influence in the establishment of the CIR in Jacksonville, provided valuable insight into his firm's pro bono work in this case and others involving wrongful convictions.

Police officer John Zipperer was first on the scene and provided a detailed account of his actions and involvement with the case as well as his perspective on the exoneration more than four decades later. Gratitude and appreciation to Zipperer (Zip) for his forty-five years of dedication to law enforcement and for putting his life on the line in service to the community.

Many thanks to Professor and former dean LeRoy Pernell of the Florida A&M Law School for his critique of the manuscript and offering a global perspective on the issue of wrongful convictions and providing resources on legal foundations.

Thank you to others interviewed for this book, including Rose Myers, Leatrice Carter, and Dick Kravitz.

Many others contributed by reading and editing initial drafts, offering advice and suggestions, including Evan Yegelwel, Alan Mizrahi, Sam Horovitz, and Mindy Horovitz.

A special thank-you to Sian Hunter, Senior Acquisitions Editor at University Press of Florida, for her support and advice. Much appreciation to Susan Murray for her expert copyediting assistance, and to the team at University Press of Florida, including Eleanor Deumens, Rachel Doll, and especially Larry Leshan, for his book cover design.

The author is grateful for all of the resources, periodicals, and public documents and would like to acknowledge the excellent work of other reporters cited in the chapter text and notes.

Finally, to my wife, Edith, who contributed to virtually every aspect of this book. You will always be the love of my life.

Appendix A

IN THE CIRCUIT COURT OF THE FOURTH JUDICIAL CIRCUIT IN AND FOR DUVAL COUNTY, FLORIDA

STATE OF FLORIDA,
Plaintiff,
Case No. 1976-CF-000912
HUBERT NATHAN MYERS,
Defendant-Movant

ORDER VACATING DEFENDANT'S JUDGMENT AND SENTENCES

THIS CAUSE, having come to be heard upon the Defendant's Motion for Postconviction Relief and to Vacate Judgment and Sentence Pursuant to Fla. R. Crim. P. 3.850, filed on March 28, 2019, and based on the State consenting to the entitlement to relief, the Court finds sufficient cause to grant the requested relief in this matter. The Court makes the following findings:

(1) The Defendant, HUBERT NATHAN MYERS, was convicted of First-Degree Murder and Attempted First-Degree Murder on September 2, 1976, and was sentenced to concurrent sentences of life imprisonment and 30 years imprisonment on October 27, 1976;

(2) In January 2018, the State Attorney's Office for the Fourth Judicial Circuit created the Conviction Integrity Review Division (CIR) to investigate and review claims of actual innocence and make recommendations on appropriate relief;

(3) The CIR performed a comprehensive and thorough review in the instant case, and performed additional investigation not previously available to this Court, the parties or the original jury;

(4) On February 25, 2019, the CIR tendered its report to counsel for the Defendant, in which it found that:

    a. Available and new evidence contradicted the State's trial theory and its only material fact witness from trial;

    b. Another man confessed to a number of people that he committed the shooting by himself, and independent investigative evidence available at the time of trial confirmed that he was present at the scene at the time of the shooting; and

    c. Multiple alibi witnesses recalled being with both the Defendant and his co-Defendant at a nearby party at the same time they heard the shots fired during the crime, demonstrating the innocence of both defendants.

(5) The CIR Report recommended that the Defendant's convictions and sentences be vacated, concluding that a "jury presented with the evidence known by the CIR could not conclude, beyond a reasonable doubt, that either defendant committed the shooting and murder," and that there "is no credible evidence of guilt, and likewise, there is credible evidence of innocence."

(6) On March 28, 2019, the Defendant filed a Motion for Postconviction Relief alleging that both the conclusions and recommendation on relief contained in the CIR Report, and certain new information produced by the CIR investigation, are newly discovered evidence upon which his convictions and sentences should be vacated.

(7) The State has consented to this Court granting the relief sought in the Motion for Postconviction Relief and stipulated that, upon issuance of this Order, it will file a Notice of Nolle Prosequi, dropping pending charges in this matter and effectuating the Defendant's immediate release from custody.

(8) This Court finds that the contents and findings contained in the CIR report support relief being granted.

(9) It is well settled that a court may grant a new trial based on newly discovered evidence if (1) the evidence was discovered since the former trial; (2) the party used due diligence at the time of trial to find such evidence; (3) the evidence is material to the issue; (4) the evidence goes to the merits and does not merely impeach the character of a witness; (5) the evidence is not merely cumulative; and (6) the evidence is such as to probably change the outcome of the trial. Smith v. state, 158 so. 91, 93 (Fla. 1934).

(10) The evidence discovered since the former trial of the sound experiment and the crime reconstruction report, evidence that the person who confessed to the crime was actually at the scene at the time of

the shooting, evidence that there was a witness at the time of the shooting who saw a single shooter outside the bedroom window, expert computer modeling which shows the wound path back to the bedroom window, is indeed material and goes directly to the merits of the case.

This evidence is not merely cumulative.

(11) The Court's role is to interpret the law; however, that interpretation is founded on the principles of justice. Justice is the paramount, indeed the exclusive interest, which concerns us. See Jackson v. State, 416 So. 2d 10, 10 (Fla. 3d DCA 1982). In this case, justice requires that a jury, if the State proceeds on this case, should hear the evidence before the Defendant may be convicted and imprisoned for the crimes with which he is charged.

(12) Thus, the newly discovered evidence is of such a nature that would probably produce an acquittal on retrial. See Jones v. State 591 So. 2d 911, 915-16 (Fla. 1991).

Accordingly, it is hereby

ORDERED that the Judgment and Sentences entered against the Defendant on October 27, 1976 in the above-referenced case number are hereby VACATED.

DONE AND ORDERED, at Jacksonville, Duval County, Florida on this 28th day of March, 2019.

Appendix B

DNA Exonerations in the United States (1989–2020)

Source: The Innocence Project

Fast Facts

1989: The first DNA exoneration took place.

375 DNA exonerees to date.

37: States where exonerations have been won.

14: Average number of years served.

5,284: Total number of years served.

26.6: Average age at the time of wrongful conviction.

43: Average age at exoneration.

21 of 375 people served time on death row.

44 of 375 pled guilty to crimes they did not commit.

69%: Involved eyewitness misidentification and of these:

34% of these misidentification cases involved an in-person lineup.

52% involved a misidentification from a photo array.

7% involved a misidentification from a mugshot book.

16% involved a misidentification from a show-up procedure.

5% involved a misidentification from a one-on-one photo procedure.

27% involved a misidentification through the use of a composite sketch.

11% involved a voice misidentification.

2% involved a misidentification through hypnosis.

54% involved an in-court misidentification.

29% involved a misidentification through some other procedure (e.g., mistakenly "recognizing" someone on the street and reporting them to law enforcement).

77% of the misidentification cases involved multiple procedures.

84% of the misidentification cases involved a misidentification by a surviving victim.

42% involved a cross-racial misidentification.

32% involved multiple misidentifications of the same person by different witnesses.

18% involved a failure to identify the exoneree in at least one procedure.

43%: Involved misapplication of forensic science.

29%: Involved false confessions.

49% of the false confessors were 21 years old or younger at the time of arrest.

31% of the false confessors were 18 years old or younger at the time of arrest.

9% of the false confessors had mental health or mental capacity issues, known at trial.

17%: Involved informants.

268: DNA exonerees compensated.

190: DNA exonerations worked on by the Innocence Project.

165: Actual assailants identified. Those actual perpetrators went on to be convicted of 154 additional violent crimes, including 83 sexual assaults, 36 murders, and 35 other violent crimes while the innocent sat behind bars for their earlier offenses.

Demographics of the 375

225 (60%) African American

117 (31%) Caucasian

29 (8%) Latinx

2 (1%) Asian American

1 (<1%) Native American

1 (<1%) Self-identified "Other"

Other Facts

130 DNA exonerees were wrongfully convicted for murders; 40 (31%) of these cases involved eyewitness misidentifications and 81 (62%) involved false confessions [as of July 9, 2018].

102 DNA exonerations involved false confessions; the real perp was identified in 76 (75%) of these cases. These 38 real perps went on to commit 48 additional crimes for which they were convicted, including 25 murders, 14 rapes, and 9 other violent crimes [as of July 24, 2018].

180 of the DNA exonerees (50%) had the real perpetrator(s) identified in their cases [as of August 22, 2018].

137 of the DNA exonerees had the real perpetrator(s) identified through a cold database hit [as of October 19, 2018].

At least 43 (52%) of the 83 DNA exonerees who falsely confessed included non-public facts in their confessions [as of July 29, 2020].

23 (22%) of the 104 people whose cases involved false confessions had exculpatory DNA evidence available at the time of trial but were still wrongfully convicted [as of July 29, 2020].

83 (61%) of the 137 DNA exonerees who were wrongfully convicted for murder had false confessions involved in their cases (33 confessed themselves, 20 had co-defendants who confessed, and another 30 confessed themselves *and* had co-defendants who confessed) [as of July 29, 2020].

Notes

Chapter 1: Introduction

1   Office of the State Attorney for the Fourth Judicial Circuit, press release, March 28, 2019, https://www.sao4th.com/conviction-integrity-williams-myers/.

2   National Registry of Exonerations, https://www.law.umich.edu/special/exoneration/Pages/about.aspx.

3   Claire Goforth, "Melissa Nelson: Folio Weekly's 2016 Person of the Year," *Folio Weekly Magazine,* December 28, 2016.

4   Ibid.

5   Ibid.

6   Amy Sherman, "Florida Has the Most Errors and Exonerations from Death Row," *Politifact,* May 27, 2014, https://www.politifact.com/factchecks/2014/jun/02/aclu-florida/florida-aclu-says-state-has-most-errors-and-exoner/.

7   National Registry of Exonerations, https://www.law.umich.edu/special/exoneration/Pages/about.aspx.

8   Equal Justice Initiative, https://eji.org/issues/wrongful-convictions/.

9   David Sheff, "Oprah Believes He's Innocent: I Hope the Court Will Agree: Free the Buddhist on Death Row," *USA Today,* November 25, 2022.

10 Ibid.

11 Equal Justice Initiative, https://eji.org/issues/wrongful-convictions/.

12 Ibid.

13 Ibid.

14 Equal Justice Initiative, https://eji.org/cases/walter-mcmillian/.

15 Box Office Mojo, https://www.boxofficemojo.com/release/rl419792385/.

16 Kate Storey, "'When They See Us' Shows the Disturbing Truth about How False Confessions Happen," *Esquire,* June 1, 2019, https://www.esquire.com/entertainment/a27574472/when-they-see-us-central-park-5-false-confessions/.

17 Samuel R. Gross, Maurice Possley, and Klara Stephens, "Race and Wrongful Convictions in the United States," National Registry of Exonerations, March 7, 2017, https://www.law.umich.edu/special/exoneration/Pages/Race-and-Wrongful-Convictions.aspx.

18 Ibid.

19 Equal Justice Initiative, https://eji.org/issues/wrongful convictions/.

20 John Grisham, "Eight Reasons for America's Shameful Number of Wrongful Convictions," *Los Angeles Times,* March 11, 2018.

21 Betsy G. Ramos, "Appellate Division Upholds Jury Verdict Against Plaintiff for Trip over a Curb," *New Jersey Litigation Blog,* November 12, 2021, https://njlitigationblog .com/appellate-division-upholds-defense-jury-verdict-against-plaintiff-for-trip -over-a-curb/.

22 LeRoy Pernell, phone interview by author, June 16, 2022.

Chapter 2: Consolidation

1 Jessie-Lynne Kerr, "A Look Back: How the Vote for Consolidation Defined Jacksonville," jacksonville.com, August 9, 2010, https://www.jacksonville.com/story/news/ 2010/08/09/vote-defined-jacksonville/15935478007/.

2 "Bold New City of the South: The Story of Jacksonville's Consolidation," *The Coastal,* August 29, 2018, https://thecoastal.com/flashback/bold-new-city-of-the-south-the -story-of-jacksonvilles-consolidation/.

3 James C. Rinaman Jr., "Outline of the History of Consolidated Government in Jacksonville, Florida," April 2013, https://www.coj.net/city-council/docs/consolidation -task-force/consolidation-history-rinaman.aspx.

4 Ibid.

5 Paul C. McCartney, Instagram.com, https://www.instagram.com/p/CBEL1QbHo PM/?utm_source=ig_embed.

6 Emily Bloch, "Why the Paul McCartney Shoutout in Jacksonville's RNC Video Raised Some Eyebrows," *Florida Times-Union,* July 5, 2020.

7 "Bold New City of the South."

8 Ibid.

9 Kerr, "A Look Back."

10 "Bold New City of the South."

11 A. G. Gancarski, "Jacksonville Mayors Talk Highs and Lows of Consolidation," FloridaPolitics.com, September 19, 2018, https://floridapolitics.com/archives/ 275239-jacksonville-mayors-talk-highs-and-lows-of-consolidation/.

12 Nate Monroe, "Consolidation: Hope vs. Reality," Jacksonville.com, September 14, 2018, https://www.jacksonville.com/story/special/special-sections/2018/09/15/to -those-left-behind-consolidated-government-is-not-all-its-cracked-up-to-be/ 10239340007/.

13 Ibid.

14 Nate Monroe, "The Broken Promise That Broke Jacksonville," *Florida Times-Union,* June 4, 2020.

15 Nate Monroe, "Two Cities, Two Epidemics," *Florida Times-Union,* April 19, 2020.

16 Ibid.

Chapter 3: Boomerang

1 Clifford Williams, interview by author, Jacksonville, Florida, February 4, 2020.

2 Ibid.

3 Ibid.

4 Ibid.

5 Tim Gilmore, "LaVilla: Perk and Loretta's Soul Lounge," Jax Geo Psycho, September 18, 2013, https://jaxpsychogeo.com/the-center-of-the-city/lavilla-perk-and-lorettas-soul-lounge/.
6 "Ax Handle Saturday," Florida Historical Society, https://myfloridahistory.org/frontiers/article/32.
7 Williams, interview.
8 Ibid.
9 Ibid.
10 Andrew Pantazi, "Anatomy of a Wrongful Conviction," *Florida Times-Union*, March 29, 2019.
11 Williams, interview.
12 Pantazi, "Anatomy of a Wrongful Conviction."
13 Williams, interview.
14 Ibid.
15 Ibid.
16 Ibid.
17 Ibid.
18 Ibid.
19 Ibid.
20 Ibid.
21 Ibid.
22 Pantazi, "Anatomy of a Wrongful Conviction."
23 Williams, interview.
24 Nathan Myers, interview by author, Orlando, Florida, August 25, 2019.
25 Ibid.
26 Ibid.
27 Ibid.
28 Ibid.
29 Ibid.
30 Ibid.
31 Ibid.
32 Ibid.

Chapter 4: Murder

1 Williams, interview.
2 George Farrar, "Jax 76," YouTube, November 11, 2017, 7:05 to 7:25, https://www.youtube.com/watch?v=DZmN5Qg5oKM.
3 Office of the Sheriff Jacksonville, *Annual Report 1976*, 8.
4 Ibid.
5 Jessie-Lynne Kerr, "Dale G. Carson, Obituary," *Florida Times-Union*, May 28, 2000.
6 Ibid.
7 Office of the Sheriff Jacksonville, *Annual Report 1976*, 21.
8 Pantazi, "Anatomy of a Wrongful Conviction."
9 Office of the Sheriff Jacksonville, *Annual Report 1976*, 26.

10 Conviction Integrity Investigation, State of Florida v. Hubert Nathan Myers, State of Florida v. Clifford Williams, Jr., State Attorney's Office, Fourth Judicial Circuit of Florida, March 26, 2019, 7; hereafter cited as CIR Report.

11 Ibid.

12 Nathan Myers, interview, August 2019.

13 CIR Report, 8.

14 Ibid., 11.

15 Ibid., 8.

16 Nathan Myers, interview, August 2019.

17 CIR Report, 8.

18 Nathan Myers, interview, August 2019.

19 Ibid.

20 John Zipperer, phone interview by author, August 18, 2020.

21 Ibid.

22 Ibid.

23 Ibid.

24 Jacksonville Sheriff's Office, *Narrative Continuation Report* (hereafter cited as NCR) 260140, July 8, 1976, 2.

25 CIR Report, 8–9.

26 Ibid., 11.

27 Krista A. Dolen, Seth E. Miller, Innocence Project of Florida, *State of Florida v. Hubert Nathan Myers,* "Defendant's Motion for Postconviction Relief," March 2019, 7.

28 CIR Report, 8, 10.

29 Jacksonville Sheriff's Office, NCR, 6.

30 CIR Report, 9.

31 Ibid.

32 Zipperer, phone interview.

33 CIR Report, 15–16.

34 Nathan Myers, interview, August 2019.

35 Ibid.

36 CIR Report, 16.

37 Ibid., 8.

38 Report of Laboratory Examination, Department of the Treasury, Bureau of Alcohol, Tobacco and Firearms, May 18, 1976.

Chapter 5: Pretrial

1 Nathan Myers, interview, August 2019.

2 John Delaney, "Delaney Has Different Take on Boonie Williams Case," *Florida Times-Union,* July 7, 2019.

3 Hank Coxe, interview by author, Jacksonville, Florida, July 15, 2021.

4 Ibid.

5 Ibid.

6 Ibid.

7 Ibid.

8 Ibid.

9 Ibid.

10 CIR Report, 25, 26.

11 Dolen and Miller, "Motion for Postconviction Relief," 4.

12 CIR Report, 26n34.

13 Dolen and Miller, "Motion for Post Conviction Relief," 4.

14 Michael A. Knox, "Forensic Analysis and Reconstruction Report," Knox & Associates, LLC, November 27, 2018, 14.

15 Dolen and Miller, "Motion for Post Conviction Relief," 4–5

16 CIR Report, 25–27.

17 Ibid., 8.

18 Jacksonville Sheriff's Office, NCR, 16.

19 Ibid., 14.

20 Ibid.

21 Ibid., 16.

22 Christie M. Letarte, "Special Master's Final Report," Florida Senate, January 23, 2020, 6.

23 Ibid.

24 Jacksonville Sheriff's Office, NCR, 16.

25 CIR Report, 31.

26 Letarte, "Special Master's Final Report," 10.

27 Ibid.

28 CIR Report, 31.

29 Ibid.

30 Ibid., 11.

31 Ibid., 37.

32 Jacksonville Sheriff's Office, NCR, 17.

33 Williams, interview.

Chapter 6: Trial and Error?

1 CIR Report, 1n2.

2 CIR Report, 41.

3 Coxe, interview.

4 CIR Report, 14n20.

5 Dick Kravitz, interview by author, Jacksonville, Florida, December 12, 2022.

6 Ibid.

7 Nathan Myers, interview, August 2019.

8 Ibid.

9 Coxe, interview.

10 Ibid.

11 Ibid.

12 Ibid.

13 Ibid.

14 Nathan Myers, interview by author, Orlando, Florida, November 3, 2021.

15 Ibid.

16 Ibid.

17 Nathan Myers, interview, August 2019.

18 Coxe, interview.

19 Nathan Myers, interview, August 2019.

20 Ibid.

21 Ibid.

22 CIR Report, 14.

23 Dolen and Miller, "Motion for Prosecution Relief," 8.

24 CIR Report, 26.

25 Ibid., 26n34.

26 Dolen and Miller, "Motion for Postconviction Relief," 8.

27 Ibid., 9.

28 CIR Report, 42.

29 Dolen and Miller, "Motion for Postconviction Relief," 11.

30 Pantazi, "Anatomy of a Wrongful Conviction."

31 Ibid.

32 CIR Report, 14.

33 The theme of quality of representation and the Sixth Amendment has been the focus of a national discourse. For context, see Strickland v. Washington, 466 U.S.668 (1984).

34 Nathan Myers, interview, August 2019.

35 Williams, interview.

36 Stephen L. Chew, "Myth: Eyewitness Testimony Is the Best Kind of Evidence," Association for Psychological Science (APS), August 20, 2018,https://www.psychologicalscience.org/teaching/myth-eyewitness-testimony-is-the-best-kind-of-evidence.html.

37 Ibid.

Chapter 7: Invest in a Vest

1 Office of the Sheriff Jacksonville, *Annual Report 1976,* 16.

2 Zipperer, phone interview.

3 Ibid.

4 Ibid.

5 Ibid.

6 Ibid.

7 Ibid.

8 Coxe, interview.

9 Zipperer, phone interview.

10 City of Jacksonville, "Jax Parks," https://www.coj.net/departments/parks-and-recreation/recreation-and-community-programming/parks/lonnie-c--miller-sr--regional-park.aspx.

11 Zipperer, phone interview.

12 Ibid.

Chapter 8: Fat Time

1 Nathan Myers, interview by author, Orlando, Florida, January 30, 2020.
2 Ibid.
3 Ibid.
4 David Reutter, "Florida's Department of Corrections: A Culture of Corruption, Abuse and Deaths," *Prison Legal News,* February 2, 2016, https://www.prisonlegalnews .org/news/2016/feb/2/floridas-department-corrections-culture-corruption-abuse -and-deaths/.
5 Nathan Myers, interview, January 2020.
6 Ibid.
7 Ibid.
8 Ibid.
9 Ibid.
10 Ibid.
11 Ibid.
12 Ibid.
13 Ibid.
14 Williams, interview.
15 Nathan Myers, interview, January 2020.
16 Ibid.
17 Ibid.
18 Ibid.
19 Ibid.
20 Ibid.
21 Ibid.
22 Ibid.

Chapter 9: Salvation

1 Nathan Myers, interview, January 2020.
2 CIR Report, 15.
3 Nathan Myers, interview, January 2020.
4 Ibid.
5 Ibid.
6 Rose Myers, interview by author, Orlando, Florida, January 30, 2020.
7 Nathan Myers, interview, January 2020.
8 Ibid.
9 Rose Myers, interview.
10 Nathan Myers, interview, January 2020.
11 Ibid.
12 Rose Myers, interview.
13 Ibid.
14 Ibid.
15 Ibid.

16 Nathan Myers, interview, January 2020.
17 Ibid.
18 Ibid.
19 Ibid.
20 Nathan Myers, interview, November 2021.
21 CIR Report, 20n29.
22 Dolen, Miller, "Motion for Postconviction Relief," 12.
23 Ibid.

Chapter 10: Confession

1 CIR Report, 20.
2 Ibid., 21.
3 Ibid., 20.
4 Tony Martin Brown, Sworn Affidavit, County of Sumter, State of Florida, October 21, 2014.
5 Ibid.
6 CIR Report, 21.
7 Ibid.
8 Ibid., 22.
9 Ibid.
10 Ibid.
11 Ibid., 23.
12 Ibid.
13 Ibid.
14 Ibid., 22.
15 Ibid., 23.
16 Ibid.
17 Ibid.
18 Ibid., 24.
19 Ibid., 21.

Chapter 11: Lightning Strikes

1 Ina Tuttle, "Angela Corey's Checkered Past," *National Review,* July 17, 2013, https://www.nationalreview.com/2013/07/angela-coreys-checkered-past-ian-tuttle/.
2 Ibid.
3 Ibid.
4 Goforth, "Melissa Nelson: Folio Weekly's 2016 Person of the Year."
5 Scott Johnson, "Alan Dershowitz vs. Angela Corey," *Powerline,* July 14, 2013, https://www.powerlineblog.com/archives/2013/07/alan-dershowitz-vs-angela-corey.php.
6 "Accused of Overcharging, Florida State Attorney Angela Corey Defends Decisions in Zimmerman, Alexander Cases," thegrio, August 1, 2013, https://thegrio.com/2013/08/01/accused-of-overcharging-florida-state-attorney-angela-corey-defends-decisions-in-zimmerman-alexander-cases/.

7 David Bauerlin, "State Attorney Angela Corey Fires Information Technology Director Who Raised Concerns in Trayvon Martin Case," *Florida Times-Union*, July 13, 2013.

8 Melissa Nelson, interview by author, Jacksonville, Florida, February 2, 2021.

9 Ibid.

10 Ibid.

11 Ibid.

12 Ibid.

13 Larry Hannan and Sebastian Kitchen, "Northeast Florida Voters Kick Controversial State Attorney Angela Corey out of Office," Jacksonville.com, August 30, 2016, https://www.jacksonville.com/story/news/politics/2016/08/30/northeast-florida-voters-kick-controversial-state-attorney-angela-corey/15722637007/.

14 Larry Hannan, "Angela Corey Snags Endorsements from Two Former Mayors," jacksonville.com, June 13, 2016, https://www.jacksonville.com/story/news/politics/2016/06/13/state-attorney-angela-corey-snags-endorsements-two-former-mayors-adds/15713587007/.

15 Hannan and Kitchen, "Northeast Florida Voters Kick Controversial State Attorney Angela Corey out of Office."

Chapter 12: Conviction Integrity

1 Buddy Schulz, interview by author, Jacksonville, Florida, November 20, 2020.

2 Ibid.

3 Innocence Project, https://innocenceproject.org/about/.

4 Patt Morrison, "Barry Scheck on the O.J. Trial, DNA Evidence and the Innocence Project," *Los Angeles Times*, June 17, 2014.

5 Ibid.

6 Innocence Project, https://innocenceproject.org/exonerations-data/.

7 "Exonerations in 2014," National Registry of Exonerations, January 27, 2015, 5, https://www.law.umich.edu/special/exoneration/Documents/Exonerations 2014.pdf.

8 Ibid.

9 "Dallas Conviction Integrity Unit Gains National Notoriety," *Prison Legal News*, July 6, 2016, https://www.prisonlegalnews.org/news/2016/jul/6/dallas-conviction-integrity-unit-gains-national-notoriety/.

10 "Justice Project," Office of Miami Dade State Attorney, https://miamisao.com/our-work/signature-programs/justice-project/.

11 Schulz, interview.

12 Ibid.

13 Nelson, interview.

14 Maurice Possley, "Jabbar Washington: Other Exonerations with Misconduct by Detective Scarcella," National Registry of Exonerations, June 15, 2020, https://www.law.umich.edu/special/exoneration/Pages/casedetail.aspx?caseid=5170.

15 Nelson, interview.

16 Dolen and Miller, "Motion for Post-Conviction Relief," 12, 13.

17 Nelson, interview.

18 Ibid.

19 Ibid.

20 Ibid.

21 Ibid.

22 Ben Conarck, "Under Melissa Nelson, Jacksonville Prosecutors Could Search for Wrongful Conviction," jacksonville.com, February 21, 2016, https://www.jacksonville.com/story/news/crime/2016/11/21/under-melissa-nelson-jacksonville-s-prosecutors-could-search-wrongful/15730047007/.

23 Nelson, interview.

24 Ibid.

25 Ibid.

26 Nathan Myers, interview, November 2021.

27 Ibid.

28 Pantazi, "Anatomy of a Wrongful Conviction."

Chapter 13: A Fox in the Henhouse

1 Nelson, interview.

2 Ibid.

3 Ibid.

4 Ibid.

5 Shelley Thibodeau, interview by author, Jacksonville, Florida, March 3, 2020.

6 Ibid.

7 Ibid.

8 Ibid.

9 Ibid.

10 Ibid.

11 Ibid.

12 Ibid.

13 Ibid.

14 Andrew Pantazi, "In a Florida First, Jacksonville's State Attorney Hired Someone to Exonerate Inmates," jacksonville.com, January 29, 2018, https://www.jacksonville.com/story/news/crime/2018/01/29/in-florida-first-jacksonvilles-state-attorney-hired-someone-to-exonerate-inmates/13985639007/.

15 Ibid.

16 Ibid.

Chapter 14: Irony

1 Thibodeau, interview, March 2020.

2 Ibid.

3 Ibid.

4 Ibid.

5 Ibid.

6 Ibid.

7 Ibid.

8 Coxe, interview.

9 "Bedell Firm Building Renovation: Before and After," *Bedell Firm News*, January 20, 2022, https://www.bedellfirm.com/bedell-firm-building-renovation-before-and -after/.

10 Coxe, interview.

11 Ibid.

12 Ibid.

13 Ibid.

14 Ibid.

15 Ibid.

16 Ibid.

17 Ibid.

18 Ibid.

19 Ibid.

Chapter 15: Reconstruction

1 Thibodeau, interview, March 2020

2 Ibid.

3 Ibid.

4 CIR Report, 17n24.

5 Shelley Thibodeau, interview by author, Jacksonville, Florida, October 20, 2021.

6 Ibid.

7 Ibid.

8 CIR Report, 16.

9 Ibid., 17.

10 Ibid., 17, 18.

11 Ibid.

12 Thibodeau, interview, March 2020.

Chapter 16: To Tell the Truth

1 Nathan Myers, interview, January 2020.

2 Thibodeau, interview, October 2021.

3 Ibid.

4 Ibid.

5 CIR Report, 25n33.

6 Thibodeau, interview, October 2021.

7 Ibid.

8 Nathan Myers, interview, January 2020.

9 Thibodeau, interview, October 2021.

10 Nathan Myers's Polygraph Examination Summary, Office of the Sheriff, Jacksonville, Florida, July 20, 2018.

11 Ibid.

12 Nathan Myers, interview, January 2020.

13 Myers's Polygraph Examination Summary.
14 Thibodeau, interview, October 2021.
15 Ibid.

Chapter 17: Shots Heard 'Round the Block

1 Thibodeau, interview, March 2020.
2 Nathan Myers, interview, November 2021.
3 Thibodeau, interview, March 2020.
4 Ibid.
5 Ibid.
6 Tom Brady, interview by author, Jacksonville, Florida, October 20, 2021.
7 CIR Report, 35, 36.
8 Ibid., 36.
9 Michael A. Knox, *Forensic Analysis and Reconstruction Report,* Knox & Associates, LLC, November 27, 2018, 17; hereafter cited as Knox Report.
10 Thibodeau, interview, March 2020.
11 Ibid.
12 CIR Report, 36.
13 Thibodeau, interview, March 2020.
14 CIR Report, 34.
15 Thibodeau, interview, March 2020.
16 CIR Report, 34.
17 Thibodeau, interview, March 2020.
18 Jim McMillan, interview by author, Jacksonville, Florida, October 5, 2021.
19 Ibid.
20 Thibodeau, interview, March 2020.
21 McMillan, interview.
22 Ibid.
23 Ibid.
24 Thibodeau, interview, March 2020.
25 McMillan, interview.
26 Ibid.
27 Ibid.
28 Ibid.
29 Ibid.
30 Jacksonville Sheriff's Office, NCR 260140, 16.
31 Thibodeau, interview, March 2020.
32 CIR Report, 33.
33 Ibid.
34 McMillan, interview.
35 Knox Report, 20.
36 Ibid., 21.
37 Ibid., 19.
38 Ibid., 23.

Chapter 18: Eyewitness?

1 CIR Report, 29.
2 Letarte, "Special Master's Final Report," 6.
3 J. Donald Jones, "Report Polygraph Examination," Associated Polygraph Consultants, Inc., July 14, 1976.
4 Ibid.
5 Ibid.
6 Ibid.
7 Ibid.
8 Ibid.
9 CIR Report, 30.
10 Dolen and Miller, "Motion for Postconviction Relief," 33, 34.
11 Ibid., 33.
12 Ibid., 33, 34.
13 Thibodeau, interview, October 2021.
14 CIR Report, 20–21.
15 Dolen and Miller, "Motion for Postconviction Relief," 37.
16 Ibid.
17 Thibodeau, interview, October 2021.
18 CIR Report, 24.
19 Ibid., 25.
20 Brown, "Sworn Affidavit."
21 Thibodeau, interview, October 2021.
22 CIR Report, 12–13.
23 Thibodeau, interview, October 2021.
24 CIR Report, 12n17.

Chapter 19: Audit

1 Thibodeau, interview, October 2021.
2 Ibid.
3 Ibid.
4 CIR Report, 40–42.
5 Thibodeau, interview, October 2021.
6 CIR Report, 43. The audit committee members were Jon Phillips, Ray Reid, Darnell
   Smith, Bill White, and Jim Casey.
7 Ibid.
8 Pantazi, "Anatomy of a Wrongful Conviction."
9 CIR Report, 43.
10 Ibid., 44.
11 Ibid., 4.
12 Ibid., 44.
13 Ibid.

Chapter 20: Free at Last

1 Nathan Myers, interview, November 2021.
2 Ibid.
3 Ibid.
4 Thibodeau, interview, October 2021.
5 Dolen and Miller, "Motion for Postconviction Relief," 42.
6 Ibid., 26.
7 Nathan Myers, interview, November 2021.
8 Ibid.
9 Ibid.
10 Ibid.
11 Scales of Justice, "Clifford Williams & Nathan Myers Wrongfully Convicted . . . Free after 42 Years," YouTube video, 13:40, March 28, 2019, https://www.youtube.com/watch?v=Ql7YPL32ydk.
12 Ibid.
13 Ibid.
14 Ibid.
15 Andrew Pantazi, "Free at Last," Jacksonville.com, March 28, 2019, https://www.jacksonville.com/story/news/courts/2019/03/28/jacksonville-freed-years-after-wrongful-murder-conviction-first-for-florida-conviction-review-unit/5515165007/.
16 Ibid.
17 First Coast News, "Raw Video: State Attorney Nelson Speaks about Release of 2 Men Wrongfully Imprisoned," YouTube video, 15:00, March 28, 2019, https://www.youtube.com/watch?v=yPWRaJZKkxg&t=5s.
18 Ibid.
19 McMillan, interview.
20 Ibid.
21 Nathan Myers, interview, November 2021.

Chapter 21: Beware of the Stare

1 Phoebe Judge, "The Sailor's Teeth," episode 191, *Criminal*, VoxMedia, June 24, 2022.
2 Ibid.
3 Nathan Myers, interview by author, November 2021.
4 Ibid.
5 Ibid.
6 Ibid.
7 Williams, interview.
8 Leatrice Carter, interview by author, Jacksonville, Florida, February 4, 2020.
9 Times-Union Editorial Board, "Justice Has Been Done by Review Unit," *Florida Times-Union*, April 2, 2019.
10 Ibid.
11 Delaney, "Delaney Has Different Take on Boonie Williams Case."

12 Ibid.

13 Ibid.

14 Ibid.

15 Ibid.

16 Ibid.

17 Bill White, "Delaney Was Off Base in Criticism of Boonie Williams Case," *Florida Times-Union*, July 14, 2019.

18 Ibid.

19 Ibid.

20 Ibid.

21 Hank Coxe, interview by Corley Peel, NewsJax4, March 29, 2029, https://www .news4jax.com/news/2019/03/30/prosecutor-from-1976-case-weighs-in-on -overturned-convictions/.

22 Katie Coxe Fackler, "Overturned Convictions Show the Need for Reconciliation," *Florida Times-Union*, April 2, 2019.

Chapter 22: Clean Hands

1 Seth Miller, "Florida Exonerees Need to Be Fairly Compensated," *Florida Times-Union*, April 23, 2021.

2 Jeffrey Schweers, "Fla. Blocks Pay for Wronged People," *Florida Times-Union*, October 19, 2021.

3 Miller, "Florida Exonerees Need to Be Fairly Compensated."

4 Letarte, "Special Master's Final Report," 7.

5 Ibid.

6 W. Jordan Jones, "Special Master's Final Report," Florida House of Representatives, January, 8, 2020, 7.

7 Florida Channel, "2/26/2020 House Judiciary Committee Hearing," Florida House of Representatives, February 26, 2020, https://thefloridachannel.org/videos/2-26 -20-house-judiciary-committee/.

8 Ibid.

9 Carolyn Snurkowski, "RE: Hubert Nathan Myers' Application for Wrongful Incarceration Compensation," Office of the Attorney General, January 23, 2020.

10 Ibid.

11 Ibid.

12 Richard H. Martin, "RE: Hubert Nathan Myers' Application for Wrongful Incarceration Compensation," Office of the Attorney General, February 15, 2020.

13 Ibid.

Chapter 23: Epilogue

1 Nathan Myers, interview, November 2021.

2 Ibid.

3 Shelley Thibodeau, phone interview by author, January 18, 2022.

4 Dan Scanlon, "Deemed a Child Rapist for 36 Years, a Jacksonville Man Is Absolved in a Case of Mistaken Identity," *Florida Times-Union*, May 22, 2022, https://www.jacksonville.com/story/news/courts/2022/05/20/Jacksonville-man-absolved-he-deemed-child-rapist-decades/9847029002/.

5 Jenese Harris, "Advocacy Group Stands behind Work after Man Who Had 1986 Conviction Vacated Accused in Recent Shooting," News4 Jax, June 28, 2022, https://www.news4jax.com/news/local/2022/06/28/advocacy-group-stands-behind-work-after-man-who-had-1986-conviction-vacated-accused-in-recent-shooting/.

6 Renee Beninate, "Man Who Spent 33 Years in Prison Back behind Bars, Now Charged with Attempted Murder," News4Jax, June 28, 2022, https://www.news4jax.com/news/local/2022/06/28/man-freed-after-33-years-in-prison-back-behind-bars-charged-with-attempted-murder/.

7 Schweers, "Fla. Blocks Pay for Wronged People."

8 Ibid.

9 National Registry of Exonerations, https://www.law.umich.edu/special/exoneration/Pages/Conviction-Integrity-Units.aspx.

10 Ibid.

11 Barry Scheck, "Conviction Integrity Units Revisited," *Ohio State Journal of Criminal Law* (2017): 750.

12 Tom Jackman, "Arrested as Teens, Three Men Exonerated after 36 Years behind Bars for Wrongful Murder Conviction," *Washington Post*, November 25, 2019.

13 Ibid.

14 National Registry of Exonerations, https://www.law.umich.edu/special/exoneration/Pages/Conviction-Integrity-Units.aspx.

15 McMillan, interview.

16 Ibid.

17 National Registry of Exonerations, "25,000 Years Lost to Wrongful Convictions," June 14, 2021, https://www.law.umich.edu/special/exoneration/Documents/25000%20Years.pdf.

18 Ibid.

19 Ibid.

20 Max Marbut, "The Federal Bar Association Jacksonville Chapter Presents the Spirit of Giving Awards," *Jacksonville Daily Record*, December 19, 2022, https://www.jaxdailyrecord.com/article/attorneys-recognized-for-community-service.

21 Nathan Myers, interview, November 2021.

22 Ibid.

Index

compensation for wrongful incarceration, 111; on Conviction Integrity Review unit, 68, 69, 70, 71, 72, 107; on denial of compensation for Nathan Myers, 113; on exoneration of Nathan Myers and Clifford Williams, 107–8; on inequality in Jacksonville, FL, 9; on Melissa Nelson, 58, 68, 69, 70, 71, 107; on Shelley Thibodeau, 72
Florida Victims of Wrongful Compensation Act, 113
Foxx, Jamie, 5

Georgetown University, 22
Georgia Tech, 14
Gibson, Audrey, 112
Gilmore, Tim, 11
Glover, Nat, 8
Good-Earnest, Margaret, 34
Gordon, Tony, 92–93
Grisham, John, 6

Hamilton Correctional Institution, 41
Harlem, NY, 12
Harrison, James, 21, 22, 28, 30, 32, 34
Harward, Keith, 105
Hillsborough County, FL, 117
Holland & Knight, 3, 54, 65, 101–2
Hollway, John, 68, 73
Holmes, Sidney, 117
Horne, Robert, 21
Howard, Ron, 8
Huckabee, Mike, 55

Innocence Project: as advocacy group, 4; Barry Scheck and, 65, 118; and Conviction Integrity Units, 66; founding of, 65; impact of O. J. Simpson trial on, 65; John Grisham and, 6; Melissa Nelson and, 66–67, 68; mission of, 65; and Myers-Williams murder case, 4; Peter Neufeld and, 65; research by, 35; retreat held by, for exonerated defendants, 115; statistics on exonerations by, 126–28; successes of, 66
Innocence Project of Florida: as branch of Innocence Project, 66; and Edward Clayton Taylor case, 116; and exoneration of Nathan Myers, 3, 111, 113; and Robert DuBoise case, 117; and Sidney Holmes case, 118
Islam, 44, 46

Jacksonville, FL: and coronavirus pandemic, 9; crime in, 1, 9, 11, 16, 17, 34, 54, 57, 78, 85; Ed Austin in, 22, 53; general counsels to, 22; government in, 7, 8–10, 16–17; and inequality, 9; inner city of, 8, 9, 10, 16; James Harrison in, 22; libraries in, 76; location of, 7; Mayo Clinic and, 8; mayors of, 22, 53, 57, 107; neighborhoods of, 9, 11, 12, 14, 17, 34, 47–48, 49, 50, 78, 85; NFL and, 8; PGA Tour and, 8; and poverty, 9; public defenders in, 22, 56; public schools in, 7; public services in, 9, 16; and race, 7–9, 10, 11–12; reputation of, 8; size of, 7; tax base of, 7, 8; and US Bicentennial, 16; and white flight, 7. *See also* Florida State Attorney's Office, 4th Judicial Circuit
Jacksonville Bar Association, 75
Jacksonville Jaguars, 76
Jacksonville Memorial Coliseum, 19
Jacksonville Sheriff's Office: in 1976, 16–17; and Baldie Williams murder, 19; and bulletproof vests, 36, 37; and Edward Clayton Taylor, 116; and Hank Coxe, 23; Intelligence Unit of, 37; Jim McMillan (father) and, 88; Jim McMillan (son) and, 87; Michael Knox and, 85–86; and polygraph of Nathan Myers, 82, 83–84; Real-Time Crime Camera of, 116
Jacksonville University, 9
Jackson v. State, 125
Jones, J. Donald, 93
Jones, Rachel: birthday party of, 18, 19, *60, 61,* 78, 80, 86, 90, 95; location of apartment of, 18, *60, 61,* 86; neighbor of, 80; sexuality of, 18
Jones, W. Jordan, 112
Jones v. State, 102
Jordan, Michael B., 5
Judge, Phoebe, 105
Justice Project, 66
Just Mercy (Stevenson), 5

BRUCE HOROVITZ is an award-winning author, journalist, and entrepreneur with extensive experience in the non-profit and business community. His book, *Gamble Rogers: A Troubadour's Life* (UPF 2018), was the recipient of the Charlton Tebeau Award from the Florida Historical Society and a Bronze Medal from the Florida Book Awards. Horovitz lives with his family in Jacksonville, FL, where he serves on several non-profit boards.